Steinbeck's
bitter fruit

Steinbeck's bitter fruit

from The Grapes of Wrath to Occupy Wall Street

Thomas Fensch

New Century Books

New Century Books
8821 Rockdale Rd.
Chesterfield, Va., 23236-2150
Newcentbks@gmail.com

Cover design and typesetting by Sun Editing & Book Design,
suneditwrite.com

Steinbeck photo: from E-bay, no photographer or date listed.

The author is grateful to the following organizations which
have granted rights to reprint copyrighted material:

Material from The Grapes of Wrath by John Steinbeck,
copyright 1939 renewed © 1967 by John Steinbeck. Used by
permission of Viking Penguin, a division of Penguin Group
(USA) Inc.;

Articles from The Huffington Post reprinted with permission;

The article "Pre-Occupied," Copyright © 2011 Conde Nast.
All rights reserved. Originally published in The New Yorker.
Reprinted by permission;

Timeline from Wikipedia and other sources;

Material from the National Center on Family Homelessness
reprinted with permission.

This book is for Robert Bonazzi, with gratitude ...

Contents

Introduction:
Steinbeck ... and Faulkner

IN 1936, JOHN STEINBECK published *In Dubious Battle*, a novel based on union organizing attempts and subsequent—and often violent—anti-union backlashes in the rich and fertile agricultural lands of California's central valleys.

He was then asked by the editors of the now-defunct *San Francisco News* to write a series of articles about the plight of the migrants, refugees from Oklahoma and other Dust Bowl states, flooding into California by the hundreds of thousands. Steinbeck's seven-part series, later re-published in book form as *The Harvest Gypsies*, was a savage indictment of conditions in California and the treatment of what some simply called "fruit tramps," once-proud Okies then resigned to doing nothing more than day-to-day crop picking.

Steinbeck used the factual articles from his *San Francisco News* series in his epic novel, *The Grapes of Wrath*. After two false starts, he finally found his focus and began *The Grapes of Wrath*; his articles from the *San Francisco News* were inserted into his novel to *prove*, to *validate*, his fiction. The title (suggested by Steinbeck's wife) came from a phrase in Julia Ward Howe's "Battle Hymn of the Republic." Lyrics from that hymn were printed on the end papers of the first edition of *The Grapes of Wrath*, published in 1939.

The themes in each are vividly apparent—and vitally important:

Union organizing activity and anti-union sentiment in *In Dubious Battle*;

Poverty and literal starvation in the *San Francisco News* series;

Homelessness, joblessness, hunger, poverty, discrimination and the greed of the banks in *The Grapes of Wrath*. Indeed, the Joads could not really comprehend why they were thrown off their Oklahoma farm. Even as meager as the topsoil was, it was *their* land—*their* dirt—*their* soil. Except it wasn't—it belonged to the bank, an inhumane creature somewhere far out of their reach. They couldn't reason with *the bank*; couldn't negotiate with *the bank*; couldn't even find a human representative of *the bank*.

And so the Joads by the thousands piled into jalopies and trucks of all sorts, many barely running, and trekked to California, the land of sun and oranges, except the California of the 1930s was a cruel hoax—the Joads found crop picking day wages so low they could not feed and support themselves.

That was John Steinbeck's 1930s.

And no one, in California, in Washington, D.C., or elsewhere, had a clue how the Great Depression would end. It finally did—on December 7, 1941—when Japan attacked the Pacific fleet in Pearl Harbor. "A day that will live in infamy," President Franklin Roosevelt called it the next day, when Congress declared war on Japan. Every man and woman who was physically able entered the armed services; plants appeared across the nation to supply war materiel; automotive assembly lines were re-tooled to build tanks, aircraft and other much needed armament. Suddenly workers were needed everywhere.

By the end of the war in 1945, old antagonisms were often—but not always—forgotten. But comparatively few of the Dust Bowl refugees ever returned to the mid-west.

That was then.

Now—73 years after Steinbeck published *The Grapes of Wrath*—we have joblessness, homelessness, poverty in America, some starvation (although we hope, not as pervasive as during Steinbeck's day) and the greed of the banks.

All back with a vengeance.

The articles in the second half of this book—and these are but a sample; there are many, many more such articles—reveal how close we may be now to Steinbeck's moral vision of the 1930s.

As examples: Republican Governors and Republican legislatures in Wisconsin and Ohio passed anti-union labor bills in 2011, only to discover they vastly over-reached. Residents in Wisconsin mounted a massive voter-recall petition to force Governor Scott Walker out of office; voters in Ohio also mounted a massive voter recall petition; they could not so easily ouster Ohio Governor John Kasich, but could vote to void the Ohio anti-union laws.

The major banks and the stock market very nearly brought economic ruin to the country in 2008 and the nation has yet to recover. More and more homes are "underwater"—homeowners owe more than their homes are worth. Many homeowners throughout the country have simply walked away from their mortgages and abandoned their homes.

Joblessness rose; poverty rose; finally Occupy Wall Street simply appeared and grew and grew; across the country and, in fact, around the world.

Since Google is now a verb, you can *google* Occupy Wall Street and find screen after screen of articles about Occupy Wall Street—its growth, implications, and future.

Would John Steinbeck of the late 1930s approve of Occupy Wall Street? I suspect we can safely say so. Would he really be surprised at the homelessness, joblessness, poverty, hunger and the greed of the banks today? It is all as he saw it then—only the year dates have changed.

And where is novelist William Faulkner in all this? In one simple and succinct quotation:

The past is never dead. It's not even past.

John Steinbeck's moral vision of the 1930s

Mine eyes have seen the glory of the coming of the Lord;
He is tramping out the vintage where the grapes of wrath
are stored;
He hath loosed the fateful lightning of his terrible quick sword:
His truth is marching on.

— Battle Hymn of the Republic
Julia Ward Howe

printed on the end papers of The Grapes of Wrath, *1939*

One |

In Dubious Battle

JOHN STEINBECK WAS BORN in Salinas, California, February 27, 1902. He attended Stanford University, sporadically from 1919-1925, taking courses in Marine Biology and literature but failed to graduate. He held various jobs including working in a sugar factory in Salinas, as a caretaker of an estate in Lake Tahoe and eventually traveled to New York City to work, building the original Madison Square Garden. He also got a job as a reporter on the old *New York American*.

He was hopelessly out of his element. "They gave me stories to cover in Queens ..." he later said, "... and Brooklyn and I would get lost and spend hours trying to find my way back." He became emotionally attached to the individuals he was supposed to be writing about; the editors transferred him to the federal courts beat, but that was even worse—Steinbeck had little knowledge of the courts system. He was fired. He attempted

1

free-lancing in New York with little success and returned to California by freighter in early 1926.

He began publishing novels in 1929, just as the Great Depression hit. His first three, which were commercial failures, were all published by firms which ultimately went bankrupt. Steinbeck's first novel, *Cup of Gold*, a fictionalized biography of the pirate Henry Morgan, was published by the firm of Robert M. McBride & Co. Lewis Gannett, the critic, wrote that his first book sold only 1,533 total copies, because few critics bothered to review it when it was published, two months after the beginning of the Great Depression.

His second book, *The Pastures of Heaven*, did little better. Published in 1932 by the firm Brewer, Warren and Putnam, it earned Steinbeck $400. Neither his first nor third book earned more than the publisher's advance of $250.

Although Steinbeck probably did not realize it at the time, 1933 marked the beginning of his sustained success as a professional, salable writer. He published two short stories, which would later become parts of *The Red Pony*, and his third book, *To a God Unknown*, found a publisher, this time the firm of Robert O. Ballou, in New York, but only 598 copies were bound and shipped to bookstores.

Then his luck began to change. Pascal Covici, a Chicago bookseller and publisher chanced to read his first three books and decided to publish Steinbeck. One of the first books Steinbeck remembered reading as a child was a version of the King Arthur stories. He became enchanted with the King Arthur saga throughout much of his life; his fascination led to two books,

Tortilla Flat and, much later, his own re-telling of the Arthurian saga, unfinished during his lifetime, but published posthumously in 1976, as *The Acts of King Arthur and His Noble Knights*.

Tortilla Flat, published in 1935, is a clear retelling of the King Arthur story, set in Depression-era California. The chapter titles are almost identical to the earliest versions of the King Arthur saga; Danny's house, the adventures of the *paisanos* and the dénouement of Steinbeck's novel reflects the original saga.

Tortilla Flat was an immediate hit for Steinbeck's new publisher, Pascal Covici. It allowed the firm Covici-Friede some welcome financial breathing room. The book won the annual Gold Medal awarded by the Commonwealth Club of California for the best work by a native Californian. The film rights were sold and eventually resold before the film version was ever made. (MGM released the film version of *Tortilla Flat* in 1942. In the book *Steinbeck and Film*, Joseph Millichamp called the film "an unreasonable sepia-toned sham that could have only been made in Hollywood.")

Readers were vastly amused (although critics ultimately less so) by Steinbeck's portrait of the *paisanos* (he had known such people in and around the Salinas-Monterey Bay area) and his mock-heroic style. Chapter nine, about the neighbor lady Sweets Ramirez and the vacuum cleaner given her as a gift, by Danny, the leader of the paisanos and his friends, shows Steinbeck at his most droll.

But once accepted as an accomplished novelist, John Steinbeck refused to be pigeon-holed and refused to follow one book with another of the same type (although he did follow *Cannery Row*, published in 1945, with the sequel *Sweet Thursday*, published in 1954).

His next book was *In Dubious Battle*, which brought him even more fame than *Tortilla Flat*. As Jackson Benson writes: "His fame grew rapidly with each book that followed—*In Dubious Battle*, *Of Mice and Men* and *The Grapes of Wrath*—in large part, of course, because the more he wrote about the things he knew, the more dynamic and convincing his work became."

Tortilla Flat and *In Dubious Battle* could not have been more dissimilar: *Tortilla Flat* is charming and engaging, especially for those who recognize the King Arthur motif. *In Dubious Battle* is cold, brutal (Steinbeck's words), detached and cynical.

Steinbeck critic Brian St. Pierre writes:

> In the mid-thirties, Salinas was in a tumult of labor unrest, as were many other agricultural areas in the state. Labor was getting organized, and so were the landowners and farmers. The Communist Party was especially active, seeing in the systemic abuse of migrant workers a golden opportunity for power. Strikes were met with brutal vigilante repression and editorial hysteria: bloodshed was all too common.
>
> Steinbeck's natural inclinations would have been to side with the oppressed anyway, but having worked in the fields gave him an especially acute view of the problems. On the other hand, he had no tolerance for the Communists, whom he felt were willing to manipulate people

and even incite violence in order to achieve their political ends.

Sometime during 1934, Steinbeck had met a Communist organizer who was on the run, hiding out in Salinas until whatever situation he'd provoked had cooled down. Steinbeck had smuggled the man some food and spent many hours in conversation with him, out of which came his short story "The Raid," which was published by *North American Review*. He thought of writing a novel that would be the biography of a Communist, then tried converting the story into a journalistic account of a strike; but it wouldn't be contained so neatly. In a letter, he wrote: "I'm not interested in strike as a means for raising men's wages, and I'm not interested in ranting about justice and oppression, mere outcroppings which indicate the condition. But man hates something in himself. He has been able to defeat every natural obstacle, but himself he cannot win over unless he kills every individual. And this self-hate which goes so closely in hand with self-love is what I wrote about. The book is brutal. I wanted to be merely a recording consciousness, judging nothing, simply putting down the thing. I think it has the thrust, almost crazy, that mobs have. It is written in disorder."

Simply stated, wages for fruit pickers were so abysmally low "fruit tramps" could work all day and not make enough to keep from starvation, let alone feed a family or travel from orchard to orchard or farm to farm seeking work. Large farms and growers' cooperatives conspired to keep wages far too low; thus leading to general labor unrest throughout California and elsewhere, during the 1930s.

Worse, as Jackson Benson writes:

> One of the tactics used by the California growers was to set one group against another, often one race against another. The Mexicans, for example, might be given a "sweetheart" contract to come in as scabs to take over from striking Filipinos or whites, or the other way around. ... at one point, growers planned to import hundreds of black pickers from the south and Mexicans from Los Angeles.

And, he also writes:

> In life, as in the fictional version, the law was usually on the side of the growers. "We protect our farmers in Kern County," said one officer. "They are our best people. They put us in here and they can put us out." Indeed, few if any of the strikers were voting residents. Many of the Mexicans were aliens, and many of the whites had come in recently from out of state. An "us versus them," or those-who-belong versus the outsiders, psychology was operative, and there were continual calls for deporting the aliens, sending the Okies back home, and getting rid of the "paid foreign agitators."

Steinbeck took the title from *Paradise Lost*:

> *Innumerable force of Spirits armed,*
> *That durst dislike his reign, and, me preferring,*
> *His utmost power with adverse power opposed*
> *In dubious battle on the plains of Heaven*
> *And shook his throne. What though the field be lost?*
> *All is not lost—the unconquerable will,*
> *And study of revenge, immortal hate,*
> *And courage never to submit or yield:*
> *And what is else not to be overcome?*

His underlying theme could also be the loss of innocence in the Garden of Eden, as the focus of the book details a strike in an orchard.

Steinbeck's publisher, Pascal Covici, very nearly turned down *In Dubious Battle*. An editor at the publishing firm wrote an in-house evaluation, stating that Steinbeck did not have the Communist tactics correctly stated in the book and that the book, if published, would be assailed by both the left and the right (which it was). Steinbeck argued to Covici that he *had* known Communist organizers in California and that reviewer's judgement was based merely on New York speculation of what organizing in the field was like. (He had, in fact, based the book in part on a strike a few years earlier near Fresno, California.) Covici relented and published the book.

Eventually, Steinbeck was disappointed that the book was often accepted as a political tract, rather than a novel. It has been ultimately recognized as the most famous labor strike novel in American literature.

And although the book is clearly about Communist labor organizing, the words Communist or "Red" or "Reds" are never used in the book; thus giving the book a universal quality—these could be any oppressed workers protesting inhumane conditions, anywhere.

Peter Lisca has offered the most succinct summary of the book:

> The novel's action begin with Jim Nolan joining "the Party" and being sent shortly afterwards into the fields with the organizer Mac as his mentor. Arriving at the migrant workers' campsite, Mac used every means to gain their confidence—even to the extent of delivering a baby. He and Jim then exploit the migrant workers' dissatisfaction with a wage cut to organize a strike, using London, the migrants' natural leader; Dakin, who owns a good truck; Sam, the most violent striker; and Burke, who turns out to be an informer, as lieutenants. The strikers are assisted by Anderson, a small grower who lets them camp on his property; Doc Burton, an uncommitted observer and commentator who directs the legally required sanitation arrangements; and Joy and Dick, fellow Communist party members. The strikers' confrontation with the three powerful growers who employ them is violent and, in the face of superior strength and the law, doomed to failure.

As they are setting up camp on Anderson's farm, a small grower who was initially in favor of the strike, Mac says to Doc:

"This is the best set-up I've seen for a long time.

"I want to work out some ideas. In don't want this ruckus to get out of hand." He gulped down some of the coffee. "Sit down on that box. we've got five acres of private property. You'll have all the help you need. Can you lay out a camp, a perfect camp, all straight lines? Dig toilets, take care of sanitation, garbage disposal? Try to figure our some way to take baths? And fill the air so God-damn full of carbolic or chloride of lime that it smells healthy? Make the whole district smell clean—can you do that?"

"Yes. I can do it. Give me enough help and I can." The sad eyes grew sadder. "Give me five gallons of crude carbolic and I'll perfume the country for miles."

"Good. Now, we're moving the men today. You look 'em over as quick as you can. See there's no contagion in any of 'em, will you? The health authorities are going to do plenty of snooping. If they catch us off base, they'll bounce us. They let us live like pigs in the jungle, but the minute we start a strike, they get awful concerned about the public health."

... the minute we start a strike, they get awful concerned about the public health ... could have been said

word-for-word about the Occupy Wall Street Zuccotti Park encampment in New York City in late 2011 and early 2012, and in other Occupy Wall Street demonstrations elsewhere throughout the United States (and abroad).

In fact, Benson writes, about a camp near Tulare California, about 1936:

> ... the growers and their sympathizers began to agitate almost immediately for the breakup of the camp, using as an excuse its dangers to the health of its inhabitants and the surrounding community. Various local officials at various times issued ultimatums to the camp demanding ten fly-tight toilets, fly-tight garbage cans, and a complex water system involving a tank, pipe lines, and numerous faucets. The irony of this sudden concern for worker health was that never were the facilities provided on the ranches subject to such scrutiny.

Later in the novel, Mac says:

> "You think we're too important, and this little bang-up is too important. If the thing blew up right now it'd be worth it. A lot of the guys have been believing this crap about the noble American working-man, an' the partnership of labor and capital. A lot of 'em are straight now. They know how much capital thinks of 'em, and how quick capital would poison them like a bunch of ants."

Eventually Joy, a Party organizer, who has been severely injured time after time by the police or vigilantes in the past, is killed by a sniper.

Readers who may believe this was too far-fetched may not know the history of those years. Jackson Benson also writes:

> ... the growers and various vigilante groups also contributed substantially to the violence: strikers were beaten, gassed and shot, and if they needed help from the authorities, they were unlikely to get it. In fact, while the growers and their friends carried guns, the strikers did not, yet it was the strikers who were almost always disciplined by the police. Farmers felt that if a striker set foot on their land or even so much as touched one of their fence posts, they were justified, under trespass law, to shoot him (or her—in life, women and children also rode in the strike caravans). In one instance, a power-company truck tried to run some pickers off the road and right of way onto private property so that the farmer, who stood by with a rifle, could shoot them. In two instances, strikers were shot and killed. Those occurrences and their aftermath are the basis for two of the most important narrative segments of *In Dubious Battle*, the killing of Joy, the old union activist, and the pageant made of his funeral.

And, at the end of the novel, Jim Nolan is killed in an ambush by a double shotgun blast, which obliterates his face.

Nolan thus becomes a martyr; the grotesque corpse is then displayed at a labor rally by Mac. The word *comrades* is used for the first and only time in the book:

London handed the lantern up, and Mac set it carefully on the floor, beside the body, so that its light fell on the head. He stood up and faced the crowd. His hands gripped the rail. His eyes were wide and white. In front he could see the massed men, eyes shining in the lamplight. Behind the front row, the men were lumped and dark. Mac shivered. He moved his jaws to speak, and seemed to break the frozen jaws loose. His voice was high and monotonous. "This guy didn't want nothing for himself—" he began. His knuckles were white, where he grasped the rail. "Comrades! He didn't want nothing for himself—"

Two |

The journalistic background of The Grapes of Wrath

IN THE EARLY 1960s, Philip Graham, then publisher of *The Washington Post*, described daily journalism as "the first rough draft of a history that will never be completed."

Graham's definition is now something of a classic, but it also applies to the background of *The Grapes of Wrath*.

Steinbeck journeyed to New York, to first work on building Madison Square Garden, then as a reporter for the *New York American*. As a reporter, Steinbeck then seemed to give a whole new meaning to the word *mediocre*. He didn't know the city, couldn't find his way around, got emotionally attached to the people he was supposed to write about dispassionately and, ultimately, had no real emotional investment in the work. He returned to California, discouraged and defeated by New York City.

How could he have done so well almost ten years later, reporting on the Okies in California, in a series published in the now long-defunct *San Francisco News*?

Here are several answers: Steinbeck had no prior experience in journalism before trekking to New York. He had studied at Stanford University, but was interested only in Marine Biology and literature. He apparently had no interest in journalism, nor did he apparently take any journalism courses.

Jump now to the 1930s. The swirling wind storms that ruined many farms in the mid-west began in this decade.

Jackson Benson's summary of the migration of the Okies describes the results of these storms:

> Their exodus from the Dust Bowl started in 1930 and increased every year, so that by 1935–1936, 87,302 entered California that year. The total number of Dust Bowl refugees that entered during that decade has been estimated at 300,000 to 400,000, an overwhelming number, considered that the total number of farm workers throughout the state prior to the influx was something over 200,000. They came with the vague idea that by heading west they might be able to get a new start, perhaps some land. But there was no land, and there was already a surplus of farm labor. At the end of Highway 66 in the Central Valley of California, they encountered an agricultural region that was probably

the most industrialized and the most highly mechanized of any such area in the world.

There these fiercely independent small farmers found themselves looked down upon. Refugees from the Bible Belt whose strict fundamentalist Christianity was an important part of their culture, they found themselves pilloried as having loose morals. A proud people who had scorned those who had accepted "charity" found themselves starving for lack of government relief. Texans who had no use for Mexicans found themselves competing with skilled Mexican field-workers for jobs, such as fruit picking and vegetable harvesting, that they knew very little about.

Californians with no ties to farming little realized the extent of the Okie invasion and much of the rest of the country also knew little about what was happening in California. (At one point, Steinbeck feared the state of California was close to a civil war—between the growers and large-scale farm owners on one side and various farm-worker minorities and Okies on the other.)

One newspaper that was aware of what was happening in the central California fruit and vegetable valleys was the *San Francisco News*. The *News* was aware of the efforts of federal administrator Tom Collins to bring cleanliness to the migrant camps which he administered. Brian St. Pierre writes:

> The first camp was built near Marysville, north of Sacramento, in 1935, and a man named

Tom Collins was chosen to run it. Collins was one of the people of whom adventure fiction is made, who turn up in a place, with a mysterious past, take hold of a difficult situation and handle it with nervy rigor and imagination, and then disappear. He not only ran labor camps, but evolved a philosophy and workable systems for them. After the Marysville camp was set up, another was built for Avrin, near Bakersfield, at the lower end of the San Joaquin Valley, and Collins moved there to run it.

One of his jobs was to keep weekly reports on doings at the camp, and he turned them into an odd literary form all his own—the most unlikely reports ever filed by a federal employee. They contained songs and poems and folk wisdom of the migrants, editorials on living conditions, journalistic accounts of life with hostile growers, and detailed inventories of the origins and possessions of the migrants.

Some of these reports were forwarded by Collins' superior to the *San Francisco News*, where they were excerpted; the *News* was a feisty Scripps-Howard newspaper and about the only one to take a stand on the plight of the workers. It was only natural that when Steinbeck got his *News* assignment, one of the first people he looked up was Tom Collins.

Few people realize, however, that Steinbeck may have been approached previously with just about the same proposal. A magazine article in the March, 1989 issue of *American Photographer* magazine was titled "Travels with Steinbeck," and sub-titled "Fifty years ago *The Grapes of Wrath* shocked the world and brought fame to its author. But few know of the photographer behind the man who wrote the novel." David Roberts writes about Horace Bristol, a California photographer who had established a studio in San Francisco and who had met Ansel Adams, Edward Weston and Dorothea Lange. By the age of 28, Bristol had been hired by *Life* magazine. Roberts writes:

> Guided by Lange, Bristol began to photograph the migrant farmers from Oklahoma who, driven from their homes by Dust Bowl drought, had flocked to California's Central Valley in a desperate search for work. He had been impressed and moved by a text-and-picture book about poverty in the south called *You Have Seen Their Faces*, a deft collaboration between photographer Margaret Bourke-White and novelist Erskine Caldwell.
>
> Bristol had a bright idea. Why not do a kindred book about Okies in California? As he pondered what writer he might persuade to compose the text, an obvious name came to mind: John Steinbeck. Bristol had never met Steinbeck, but he had read *In Dubious Battle*, a novel that flaunted Steinbeck's sympathies with organized labor. Late in 1937, Bristol recalled, "I called Steinbeck on the phone and told him what I wanted to do. He said 'come on down and we'll talk about it.'" At the novelist's cottage in

Los Gatos, Steinbeck and Bristol shared a lei-
surely lunch and two bottles of wine. Steinbeck
thought Bristol was onto something important.
He agreed to collaborate on the book.

During five or six weekends in early 1938,
the writer and the photographer drove to the
Central Valley to gather material. They traveled widely, but both men were riveted by what
they saw around the town of Visalia, where
midwinter floods were taking a grim toll among
the Okies in starvation and disease.

"Steinbeck was wonderful," recalls Bristol.
"The ease with which he worked with those
people—they never felt defensive. They just
opened up him. He'd get talking to someone,
and I'd move in behind him with the camera. "

Two or three months after their last trip to
Vasalia, Bristol called Steinbeck. "I said, 'I think
I have enough pictures.' He said, 'Well Horace, I
have bad news for you. I'm going to write it as
a novel.'"

This episode is not mentioned in Benson's *The True
Adventures of John Steinbeck, Writer*, the longest and
most comprehensive Steinbeck biography extant,
although Benson mentions that *Life* magazine published
some of Bristol's migrant photos. Robert DeMott, at the
end of the Introduction to *Working Days* (Steinbeck's
diary during the months he wrote *The Grapes of Wrath*)
refers to the Bristol-Steinbeck anecdote and cites some
additional Bristol publications clarifying his work and
his impressions of Steinbeck's work during those days.

If this Bristol episode has not been verified in all Steinbeck biographies, Steinbeck's work with Tom Collins is well known. Brian St. Pierre mentioned their collaboration in his book, *John Steinbeck: The California Years* as does Benson. St. Pierre writes:

> Most of Steinbeck's best work began with real people and first-hand observation, and in Tom Collins he had the richest imaginable source and best guide. *The Grapes of Wrath*, which eventually came out of their friendship, is dedicated to him.

Jackson Benson relates this part of Steinbeck's life:

> In preparation for his trip and in order to travel among the migrants as inconspicuously as possible, Steinbeck bought an old bakery "pie wagon" as he called it, and outfitted it with blankets, food and cooking utensils. Then in late August he went to San Francisco to talk over his assignment with the editors at the *News* and get a briefing from federal officials at the Resettlement Administration regional headquarters. He talked to Fred Soule at the Information Division and was able to gather most of the general background and statistical data he needed for his articles. The Resettlement Administration was having a hard time selling its program, and the possible favorable publicity that might come from Steinbeck's series was given high priority. He then left for a tour of the San Joaquin Valley,

accompanied by ex-preacher Eric H. Thomsen, who was Director in Charge of Management (for the migrant camp program) for Region IX.

Driving down through the Central Valley, the two men sought out and stopped at several squatters camps. Thomsen wanted to show Steinbeck the contrast between how the migrants lived on their own and how they lived at the sanitary camps provided by the government. Steinbeck had had some experience with hobo camps and labor camps, had seen the Hoovervilles that dotted the landscape and the slum filth of those encampments appalled him. And the people—beaten-down, scorned, without hope and terrified of starvation—he couldn't get them out of his mind.

So Steinbeck completed his seven-part series "The Harvest Gypsies," which was published in the *San Francisco News*, October 5-12, 1936. (And later in *The Grapes of Wrath*, he used as a key character an ex-preacher. Tom Collins was also later the technical advisor for the film version of *The Grapes of Wrath*. His name appears in the film credits.)

What can we learn from that series—and how can we judge Steinbeck's "new" attempt at journalism—after his failure a decade earlier in New York City?

"The Harvest Gypsies" is devoted (in order) to:

Article One: A General Introduction;
Article Two: The Squatters' Camp;
Article Three: The Small Farm Owner;

Article Four: The Federal Government;
Article Five: The Story of One Family;
Article Six: Foreign Labor in California;
Article Seven: Suggestions for Humane Treatment
    of the Migrants and Prognosis for the Future.

In the first article, Steinbeck begins with a panoramic lead (pronounced *leed*, a beginning, in journalism terms):

> At this season of the year, when California's great crops are coming into harvest, the heavy grapes, the prunes, the apples and lettuce and the rapidly maturing cotton, our highways swarm with the migrant workers, that shifting group of nomadic, poverty-stricken harvesters driven by hunger and the threat of hunger from crop to crop, from harvest to harvest, up and down the state and into Oregon to some extent, and into Washington a little. But it is in California which has and needs the majority of these new gypsies. It is a short study of these wanderers that these articles will undertake. There are at least 50,000 homeless migrants wandering up and down the state, and that is an army large enough to make it important to every person in the state.

Despite one awkward sentence: "It is a short study of these wanderers that these articles will undertake," Steinbeck provides not only an adequate, but an exceptional beginning to his series. One of the keys to the entire series of articles is observation: Steinbeck is a keen observer. And that is a notable characteristic not only of a reporter, but of a novelist as well. Steinbeck's series is filled with descriptive phrases, for example: "open rattletrap cars loaded with children and with dirty bedding, with fire-blacked cooking utensils."

The articles are also not inflamed. Steinbeck wants the reader to be touched by the circumstances, not his polemic. Two rules of reportage are that the reporter remains neutral and the reporter does not add emotion through the addition of punctuation such as the exclamation mark. In this series, Steinbeck's articles follow these rules.

We cannot now know how the editors of the *San Francisco News* might have edited Steinbeck's material: we have no first drafts of this series to compare with the final published versions. The newspaper does not exist today; thus we have no access to its record or file copies. Since the editors commissioned Steinbeck to write this series as a correspondent or expert—since they bought his by-line and expertise and since they left standing one awkward sentence in the beginning paragraph of the first article of the series, it is likely that they left Steinbeck's copy alone.

What journalistic shortcoming do we see in Steinbeck's "Harvest Gypsies" copy?

He includes few quotations. In the first article, he quotes an anonymous boy: "When they need us they call us migrants, and when we've picked their crop, we're bums and have to get out." At the end of the fifth article, Steinbeck offers a slightly longer quotation from a migrant mother who had just given birth to a still-born baby. (Steinbeck used both this same quotation and the still-born baby episode in *The Grapes of Wrath*.)

He highlights no individuals. Through the series, Steinbeck offers vague portraits of individual migrants. (He probably realized that picturing one migrant might have distorted the series.)

Steinbeck offers the reader composite pictures of several migrants or migrant situations he has observed.

In the first article, Steinbeck introduces the plight of the migrants in California and the extent of the problem facing all Californians—natives *and* migrants.

In the second installment of the series, Steinbeck shows us three levels of hopelessness inside the squatters' camps: the newly-arrived family, which still has some possessions, a little money and some hope of the future; the family that has lived in the camp for a year or so, living in filth and squalor, with little money and little hope; and at the third level, the family that has no hope, no money and that has succumbed to illness and death.

Steinbeck writes:

> The next door neighbor family of man, wife and three children of from three to nine years of age, have built a house by driving willow branches into the ground and wattling weeds, tin, old paper and strips of carpet against them. A few branches are placed over the top to keep out the noonday sun. It will not turn water at all. There is no bed. Somewhere the family has found a big piece of old carpet. It is

on the ground. To go to bed the members of the family lie on the ground and fold the carpet over them.

The three year old child has a gunny sack tied about his middle for clothing. He has the swollen belly caused by malnutrition.

He sits on the ground in the sun in front of the house, and the little black files buzz in circles and land on his closed eyes and crawl up his nose until he weakly brushes them away.

They try to get the mucous in the eye-corners. This child seems to have the reactions of a baby much younger. The first year he had a little milk, but he has had none since.

He will die in a short time. The older children may survive. Four nights ago the mother had a baby in the tent, on the dirty carpet. It was born dead, which is just as well because she could not have fed it at her breast; her own diet would not produce milk.

After it was born and she had seen it was dead, the mother rolled over and lay still for two days, She is up today, tottering around. The last baby, born less than a year ago, lived a week. The woman's eyes have the glazed, far-away look of a sleepwalker's eyes. She does not wash clothes any more. The drive that makes for cleanliness has been drained out of her and she hasn't the energy. The husband was a share-cropper once, but he couldn't make it go. Now he has lost even the desire to talk. He will not look directly at you, for that requires will, and will needs strength. He is a bad field worker for the same reason. It takes him a long time to make up his mind, so he is always late in moving and late in arriving in the fields. His top wage, when he can find work now, which isn't often, is a dollar a day.

The children do not even go to the willow clump any more. They squat where they are and kick a little dirt. The father is vaguely aware that there is a culture of hookworm in the mud along the river bank. But he hasn't the will nor the energy to resist. Too many things have happened to him.

Jackson Benson writes: "The family Steinbeck was writing about was actually a composite of several families he had encountered in visiting one squatters' camp after another."

The use of composite characters is dangerous in journalism because the composite character may not be an accurate representation of one individual. In Steinbeck's day such composite characters may have been tolerated in journalism —today such practices are criticized as unethical.

In the series' third part—the section devoted to the small farmer—we see a variety of journalistic elements in Steinbeck's prose. The opening sentence, "When in the course of the season the small farmer has need of an influx of migrant workers ..." sounds like the Declaration of Independence: "When in the course of human events...." Again we see Steinbeck generalizing about the small farmer—no individual farmer is pictured. Rather Steinbeck summarizes all small farmers in California. He writes:

> It is rare in California for a small farmer to be able to plant and mature his crops without loans from banks and finance companies. And since these banks and finance companies are at once members of the powerful growers' associations, and at the same time the one source of crop loans, the force of their policies on the small farmer can readily be seen. To refuse to obey is to invite foreclosure or a future denial of the necessary crop loan.

In short, Steinbeck understood the interlocking nature of the banks and the large-scale farmers: how they could destroy the small farmer who didn't comply with the migrant-labor policies imposed by the farmers' associations and banks.

Steinbeck was, for the series "The Harvest Gypsies," a true investigative reporter. He understood the policies and politics of the state and region: he could work with experts like Tom Collins; he could talk easily with migrant families; he could write well; he was an accurate observer; and, he had the physical energy and stamina to conduct extensive research.

Moreover, he did not let his outrage cripple his aims or his prose. He told the story simply and effectively.

In the third article, we even see examples of the farmer's slang—Steinbeck talks about the "pusher," the field boss in the orchards and the "pacer," a rabbit-like picker, whose productivity all migrants attempted to match. Even though, Steinbeck admits, "it is often the case that the pacer's row is done over again afterwards."

In the fourth article, Steinbeck discusses the role of the federal government in the California migrant affair. Steinbeck observes that the cost to the federal government to erect the migrant camp at Arvin was $18,000, exclusive of the cost to rent the land. (It certainly shows the difference between Steinbeck's day and our own, when we realize that today $18,000 is less than the average cost of a new car.)

In this same article, Steinbeck discusses the democratic policies in the Arvin camp—including a dramatic section on "The Good Neighbors," the women's association. Steinbeck writes:

> ... takes part in quilting and sewing projects, sees that destitution does not exist, governs and watches the nursery, where children can be left while the mothers are working in the fields and in the packing sheds. And all of this is done with the outside aid of one manager and one part-time nurse. As experiments in natural and democratic self-government, these camps are unique in the United States.

And, he writes:

> When a new family enters one of these camps, it is usually dirty, tired and broken. A group from the Good Neighbors meets it, tells it the rules, helps it get settled, instructs it in

the use of the sanitary facilities, and if there are insufficient blankets or shelters, furnishes them from its own stores.

Steinbeck even quotes the manager's logbook:

> New arrivals. Low in foodstuffs. Most of the personal belongings were tied up in sacks and were in filthy condition. The Good Neighbors at once, took the family in hand, and by 10 o'clock they were fed washed, camped, settled and asleep.

In the fifth article, Steinbeck discusses one family—again probably a composite of several families. And he discusses this family in terms of food and medical needs after their five-year-old boy was arrested for stealing a metal piece of gear to sell for food. The father had strained an ankle previously and re-injured it walking to town to free the son. The son subsequently died of a burst appendix suffered in the field and left untreated. A young daughter became ill with influenza and the family did not have enough money for a doctor. "This can go on indefinitely," Steinbeck writes. "The case histories like it be found in their (sic) thousands."

Steinbeck even cites the typical diet for migrant families:

> Family of eight—Boiled cabbage, baked sweet potatoes, creamed carrots, fried dough, jelly, tea.
> Family of seven—Beans, baking-powder biscuits, jam, coffee.

Family of six—Canned salmon, cornbread, raw onions.

Family of five—Biscuits, fried potatoes, dandelion greens, pears.

These are dinners. It is to be noticed that even in the flush times there is no milk, no butter. The major part of the diet is starch. In slack times the diet becomes all starch, this being the cheapest way to fill up. Dinners during lay-offs are as follows:

Family of seven—Beans, fried dough.
Family of six—Fried oatmeal.
Family of five—Oatmeal mush.
Family of eight (there were six children)—Dandelion greens and boiled potatoes.

And again, Steinbeck stresses childbirth:

The following is an example: wife of family with three children. She is 38, her face is lined and thin and there is a hard glaze on her eyes. The three children who survive were born prior to 1929, when the family rented a farm in Utah. In 1930 this woman bore a child which lived for four months and died of "colic."

In 1931 another child was born dead because a "han' truck fulla boxes run inta me two days before the baby come." In 2932 there was a miscarriage. "I couldn't carry the baby because I was sick." She is ashamed of this. In 1933 her baby lived a week. "jus died. I don't

know what of." In 1934 she had no pregnancy,
she is also a little ashamed of this. In 1935 her
baby lived a long time, nine months.

"Seemed for a long time like he was gonna
live. Big strong fella it seemed like." She is pregnant again. "If we could get milk for 'um I guess
it would be better."

"This is an extreme case, but by no means an unusual
one," Steinbeck writes. And we cannot but wonder if he
had the Rose of Sharon end sequence of *The Grapes of
Wrath* in mind at the time.

In the sixth article Steinbeck discusses the waves
of foreign labor which coursed through California: the
Chinese; then the Japanese; then Mexican laborers.
("By 1920 there were 80,000 foreign-born Mexicans
in California," Steinbeck writes.) Finally, Filipinos
entered California in vast numbers. Again, Steinbeck
uses statistics clearly, although his phrase "little brown
men," is clearly patronizing today. "Between 1920 and
1929, 31,000 of these little brown men were brought
into the United States, and most of them remained in
California, a new group of peon workers."

Finally, he warns discretely that the Okies, the
newest wave of labor in California, will not tolerate the
same conditions which foreign labor tolerated: "Foreign
labor is on the wane in California, and the future farm
workers are to be white and American. The fact must be
recognized and a rearrangement of the attitude toward
and treatment of migrant labor must be achieved."

In the final article, Steinbeck suggests solutions
for the problems of the Okies: since the Okies were

former farmers, land should be leased from the state or from the federal government for their use; the state should erect simple homes for their use in areas where migrant labor is needed; crop use should be changed so migrant pickers are not needed so crucially; instruction in health techniques should be made available to migrant workers and migrant labor committees should be set up to govern migrant affairs.

The California Attorney General's Office should have the power to investigate cases of vigilante terrorism throughout the state. These—and other suggestions—seem entirely logical to us in retrospect. In Steinbeck's day, these were considered radical and dangerous notions.

How do we judge Steinbeck's "Harvest Gypsies" series? He did everything well:

* The series was well conceived and planned;

* Whether the proposed book with photographer Horace Bristol is an entirely accurate anecdote about Steinbeck, Bristol correctly observed "Steinbeck was wonderful. The ease with which he worked with these people—they never felt defensive. They just opened up to him.";

* Steinbeck completely understood the underlying California politics—the interaction between the banks and the large growers;

* He worked with the right people to get information he needed, notably Tom Collins;

* He used statistics correctly in the series and even used the slang of the growers accurately;

* His anger at the injustices of the farming system in California was tempered by his style—the series was neither too sedate nor too polemical.

How do others view "The Harvest Gypsies"?

In *Working Days: The Journals of The Grapes of Wrath*, Robert DeMott says "'The Harvest Gypsies' (were) hard-hitting, unflinching investigative reports ... full of case studies, chilling factual statistics and an unsettling catalog of human woes."

When they were first published in 1936 (and again when they were printed in 1938—in pamphlet form—as *Their Blood Is Strong*), Steinbeck's articles solidified his credibility—both in and out of the migrant camps—as a serious commentator. "The Harvest Gypsies" (and Tom Collins' continuing reports) provided Steinbeck with a basic repository of precise information and folk values.

DeMott also writes:

> From his numerous field trips with Tom Collins, and from countless hours of listening to migrant people, working beside them, listening to them and sharing their problems, Steinbeck drew all the correct details of human forms, language and landscape that ensure artistic verisimilitude, as well as the subtler nuances of dialect, idiosyncratic tics, habits, and gestures, which animate fictional characterization.

So the first key to the success of *The Grapes of Wrath* is: when Steinbeck needed to be, he became a gifted reporter. Earlier, in New York City, he did not "know the terrain." But later, In California, he *did* care about the injustices of the migrant camps. He was not only an accurate observer, but he saw the meaning in human events. He was outraged at what he saw, but channeled his outrage into exceptional nonfiction, then fiction.

And how did he use the material from "The Harvest Gypsies" in *The Grapes of Wrath*?

He knew he faced a problem with the novel. He knew that when the novel appeared, critics could easily dismiss the book by saying "the Joads are purely fiction—that isn't the way it is in California at all."

So Steinbeck wove "The Harvest Gypsies" into *The Grapes of Wrath*. The articles constitute the inner-chapters (strictly speaking called *intercalary* chapters, or material inserted into a narrative). He discusses the used cars, the "jalopies," which the migrants used to drive to California; the "Good Neighbors" in the migrant camp and other factual material. How do they affect the novel? Simply stated, they serve as breaks in the narrative to give the reader some psychological distance from the characters and the plot.

Later, when producer Daryl F. Zanuck was making the film version of *The Grapes of Wrath*—with a young Henry Fonda as Tom Joad—he wanted to know that the conditions were as Steinbeck said they were. So he sent detectives out to see how truthful Steinbeck had been. When they returned, their report was: *conditions are worse than Steinbeck reported.*

Not only was Steinbeck an excellent reporter when he needed to be, he also used his facts to *prove*, to *validate* his fictional world. No critic could reasonably say *The Grapes of Wrath* was "just a novel." The Joads might be fiction; the story wasn't.

Three |

The Grapes of Wrath

THE BOOK OF EXODUS in the Bible describes the ten plagues, or calamities, that God inflicted on ancient Egypt, to persuade the Pharaoh to release the ill-treated tribe of Israel from slavery.

The ten plagues (Exodus 8-12) were:

* water, which turned to blood and killed all the fish and other aquatic life;

* frogs;

* lice;

* flies or wild animals;

* disease on livestock;

* unhealable boils;

* hail and thunder;

* locusts;

* darkness;

* and the death of the first-born of all Egyptian humans and animals. The first three seemed to affect all of Egypt, but the children of Israel were not affected by the fourth, fifth, sixth, seventh and ninth plague. To be saved from the tenth plague—the death of the first-born—the Israelites had to place the blood of a lamb on their door. The Torah describes the angel of death as actually passing through Egypt to kill all first born children but passing over (hence "Passover") houses which had the sign of lambs' blood on the doorpost. On the night of this plague, the Pharaoh finally relented and sends the Israelites away under their terms. This departure was known as the Exodus.

Whether John Steinbeck re-read Exodus or only vaguely remembered it, he may well have imagined or visualized that the horrific dust storms of the 1930s, which darkened the skies and blotted out the sun, and the subsequent barren and unproductive farmlands were two twentieth-century plagues.

In fact, *The Grapes of Wrath* is clearly a re-telling of the journey of the tribe of Israel away from their land of bondage, Egypt, toward their promised land, but *The Grapes of Wrath* is a black reversal of the biblical journey of the Jewish people. The Joads, and countless thousands of others, found they were treated more savagely in California than they ever had been in their native states.

The Grapes of Wrath is rife with biblical references; the first, the entire journey as a twentieth-century pilgrimage from a land of bondage, towards a promised land.

Other biblical references include an episode along the journey when another family stops at a truck stop to buy food. But they can only afford *a half-loaf of day-old bread.* A dime's worth of day-old bread. Their two little boys eagerly stare at a glass case of candy. The father joins them at the candy case:

> He pointed in the case at big long sticks of striped peppermint. "Is them penny candy, ma'am?"
>
> Mae moved down and looked in. "Which ones?"
>
> "There, them stripy ones."
>
> The little boys raised their eyes to her face and they stopped breathing; their mouths were partly opened, their half-naked bodies were rigid.
>
> "Oh—them. Well, no, them's two for a penny."
>
> "Well, gimme two then, ma'am."

The boys grip their pieces of candy and the family leaves. Mae, the waitress, and two truck drivers watch them disappear. One of them confronts her:

> "Them wasn't two-of-a-cent candy," he said.
>
> "What's that to you?" Mae said fiercely.
>
> "Them was nickle apiece candy," said Bill.

The two truckers get up to go back on the road, and leave a tip on the table. 'Way too much tip.

> Mae called, "Hey! Wait a minute. You got change."
> "You go to hell," said Bill, and the screen door slammed.

Some readers may miss the biblical reference in this: it was, as I always remembered it, "cast thy bread upon the waters and it will be returned tenfold." (Be generous to the least of God's children and you will be rewarded. In this case, literally the children.) The actual biblical reference is Ecclesiastes 1:11: cast thy bread upon the waters for you shall find it after many days.

An itinerant preacher Jim Casy (initials *J.C.*) had joined the Joad family in Oklahoma on their trek toward California and, much later, after they reached California, he is killed by a vigilante.

> A short heavy man stepped into the light. He carried a new white pick handle.
> Casy went on. "You don't know what you're a-doin'."
> The heavy man swung with the pick handle. Casy dodged down into the swing. The heavy club crashed into the side of his head with a dull crunch of bone, and Casy fell sideways out of the light.
> "Jesus, George," another vigilante says, " I think you killed him."

"You don't know what you're a-doin'" sounds very close to Christ's words: "Forgive them Father for they know not what they do." (Luke 23-24)

Tom Joad attacked the vigilante who was swinging the pick handle at Casy; although Tom escaped, he was on parole after a prison stint in Oklahoma. He suspected if he was identified for the assault and captured he might be returned to prison in Oklahoma and, since the Joad family was living by the barest threads in California, he might put the rest of them at risk.

He had to flee. And he had to tell his mother, who asked the most basic of maternal questions: *what are you going to do?* and *where are you going to be?*

> "Then what, Tom?"
>
> "Then it don' matter. Then I'll be around in the dark. I'll be ever'where—wherever you look. Wherever they's a fight so hungry people can eat, I'll be there. Wherever they's a cop beatin' up a guy, I'll be there. If Casy knowed, why, I'll be in the way guys yell when they're mad an'—I'll be in the way kids laugh when they're hungry an' they know supper's ready. An' when our folks eat the stuff they raise an' live in the houses they build—why, I'll be there. See? God, I'm talkin' like Casy. Comes of thinkin' about him so much. Seems like I can see him sometimes.
>
> "I don' un'erstand'," Ma said. "I don' really know."

"I'll be ever'where ..." sounds close to Christ's words, "Lo, I am with you always, even to the end of the world." (Matthew 28:20)

Rose of Sharon, the young bride, had been pregnant throughout the trip to California. Her husband had "run off," abandoning her during her pregnancy. She lacked the basic diet for a successful pregnancy: meat; milk; regular meals.

She went into labor in an empty boxcar during a flood. But her baby was stillborn. Born dead. "A blue shriveled little mummy." The Joads knew that local cemeteries would not bury Okie dead. Grandpa Joad had died during the journey and was buried in a make-shift grave at the edge of a field near the highway.

What to do? They found a sack for the little thing, and an apple packing box, used in the orchards, for a casket.

> In the gray dawn light Uncle John waded around the end of the car, past the Joad truck; and he climbed the slippery bank to the high-way. He walked down the highway, past the boxcar flat, until he came to a place where the boiling stream ran close to the road, where the willows grew along the road side. He put his shovel down, and holding the box in front of him, he edged through the brush until he came to the edge of the swift stream. For a time he stood watching it swirl by, leaving its yellow foam among the willow stems. He held the apple box against his chest. And then he

leaned over and set the box in the stream and steadied it with his hand. He said fiercely "Go down an' tell 'em. Go down in the street an' rot an' tell 'em that way. That's the way you can talk. Don' even know if you was a boy or a girl. Ain't gonna find out. Go on down now an' lay in the street. Maybe they'll know then." He guided the box gently out into the current and let it go. It settled low in the water, edged sideways, whirled around, and turned softly over. The sack floated away, and the box, caught in the swift water, floated quickly away, out of sight, behind the brush.

"Go down an' tell 'em ..." meant, of course, that if the body drifted downstream and was found, Californians would know it was an Okie baby, prohibited by local officials from burial in a local cemetery.

This is the darkest possible reversal of the biblical story of the baby Moses, found in the bulrushes by a river (Exodus 1:12:10).

And, of course, Rose of Sharon is a biblical name (Song of Solomon 2:1).

Steinbeck sometimes spent months and months on false starts and unfinished versions of his work; *The Grapes of Wrath* was no exception.

It was completed after a series of three previous steps: "The Harvest Gypsies" series in the *San Francisco News* was the first step; the second step was a project, an unfinished novel, *The Oklahomans*, abandoned and no longer extant; the third step was a completed satire, *L'Affair Lettuceburg*, (based on a Salinas, California, lettuce strike in September, 1936) which neither Steinbeck nor his wife Carol liked, and which he destroyed.

Robert DeMott writes:

> Each stage varied in audience, in intention, and tone from the one before it. All the versions overlapped, however, because they shared—with differing highlights and resolutions—a fixed core of elements: on one side, the entrenched power, wealth, authority, and consequent tyranny of California's industrialized agricultural system (symbolized by Associated Farmers, Inc.), which produced flagrant violations of the migrants' civil and human rights and ensured their continuing peonage, their loss of dignity, through threats, reprisals, and violence; on the other side, the powerlessness, poverty, victimization, and fear of the nomadic American migrants whose willingness to work, desire to retain their dignity, and enduring wish to settle land of their own were kept alive by their innate resilience and resourcefulness, and by the democratic benefits of the government sanitary camps.

Finally Steinbeck began *The Grapes of Wrath* in late May, 1938. His wife Carol supplied the title. He worked on it through the winter of 1938, finishing it at the point of a nervous breakdown.

There was ... something in his makeup that
seemed to make it impossible for him to slowly
plan, develop, and then deliberately write a long
work of fiction. The pressure of material and
emotion built up in his mind, so that once his
direction had finally been determined, he took
off like a sprinter rather than a long-distance
runner. When at last he did get into the writing of the final draft of *The Grapes of Wrath*, he
made it a long sprint, rather than a marathon
run, and the strain very nearly destroyed him.

... Jackson Benson wrote.

His visits to the migrant camps and the other
locations for "The Harvest Gypsies" had convinced
Steinbeck that he was witnessing tragedy on a massive
scale. Much later he said he had written *The Grapes of
Wrath* "protesting what I had seen ... during the migration of thousands of dispossessed families. I saw people
starve to death. That's not just a resounding phrase.
They starved to death. They dropped dead."

The Grapes of Wrath focuses on five nearly unsolv-
able problems during the Dust Bowl migration of the
1930s: homelessness; joblessness; poverty; hunger ...
and the greed of the banks.

Early in *The Grapes of Wrath*, Steinbeck writes:

The owners of the land came onto the land,
or more often a spokesman for the owners
came. They came in closed cars, and they felt
the dry earth with their fingers, and sometimes

they drove big earth augers into the ground for
soil tests. The tenants, from their sun-beaten
dooryards, watched uneasily when the closed
cars drove along the fields. And at last the
owner men drove into the dooryards and sat in
their cars to talk out of the windows. The tenant men stood beside the cars for a while, and
then squatted on their hams and found sticks
with which to mark the dust.

In the open doors the women stood looking
out, and behind them the children—corn-headed
children, with wide eyes, one bare foot on top of
the other bare foot, and the toes working. The
women and the children watched their men
talking to the owner men. They were silent.

Some of the owner men were kind because
they hated what they had to do, and some of
them were angry because they hated to be
cruel, and some of them were cold because
they had long ago found that one could not be
an owner unless one were cold. And all of them
were caught in something larger than themselves. Some of them hated the mathematics
that drove them, and some were afraid, and
some worshiped the mathematics because
it provided a refuge from thought and from
feeling. If a bank or a finance company owned
the land, the owner man said, The Bank—
or the Company—needs—wants—insists—must
have—as though the Bank or the Company
were a monster, with thought and feeling,
which had ensnared them. These last would

take no responsibility for the banks or the companies because they were men and slaves, while the banks were machines and masters all at the same time. Some of the owner men were a little proud to be slaves to such cold and powerful masters. The owner men sat in the cars and explained. You know the land is poor. You've scrabbled at it long enough, God knows.

The squatting tenant men nodded and wondered and drew figures in the dust, and yes, they knew, God knows. If the dust only wouldn't fly. If the top would only stay on the soil, it might not be so bad.

The owner men went on leading to their point: You know the land's getting poorer. You know what cotton does to the land; it robs it, sucks all the blood out of it.

The squatters nodded—they knew, God knew. If they could only rotate the crops they might pump blood back into the land.

Well, it's too late. And the owner men explained the workings and the thinkings of the monster that was stronger than they were. A man can hold land if he can just eat and pay taxes; he can do that.

Yes, he can do that until his crops fail one day and he has to borrow money from the bank.

But—you see, a bank or company can't do that, because those creatures don't breathe air, don't eat side-meat. They breathe profits; they eat the interest on money. If they don't get it, they die the way you die without air, without side-meat. It is a sad thing, but it is so. It is just so.

And, Steinbeck wrote ...

The bank—the monster has to have profits all the time. It can't wait. It'll die.... When the monster stops growing, it dies. It can't stay one size.

... and ...

Sure, cried the tenant men, but it's our land. We measured it and broke it up. We were born on it, and we got killed on it, died on it. Even if it's no good, it's still ours. That's what makes it ours—being born on it, working it, dying on it. That means ownership, not a paper with numbers on it.

We're sorry. It's not us. It's the monster. The bank isn't like a man.

Yes, but the bank is only made of men.

No, you're wrong there—quite wrong there. The bank is something else than men. It happens that every man in a bank hates what the bank does, and yet the bank does it. The bank is something more than men, I tell you. It's the monster. Men made it but they can't control it.

And so the Joads and others like them, in Oklahoma and Texas and Kansas and elsewhere, were thrown off their land and they headed for California—into a bleak and uncertain future.

Reception of *The Grapes of Wrath* when it was published plunged Steinbeck into a firestorm. Few novelists have been the recipient of so much personally directed hatred, and of all novelists, he was probably the least able to shrug his shoulders and let the venom run off his back, Jackson Benson said.

Oklahoma Congressman Lyle Boren read bitter criticism into *The Congressional Record*:

> I say to you and to every honest, square-minded reader in America, that the painting Steinbeck made in the book is a lie, a black infernal creation of a twisted, distorted mind.

One small-town Californian claimed the book was "obscene in the extreme" (although there are no obscenities in it) but later admitted he had not read the book before making that charge. The book was banned or burned in several cities including Buffalo, New York; East St. Louis, Illinois, and Kern County California, and continues to this day to be one of the most controversial books in public libraries.

Steinbeck knew that publication came with considerable personal risk:

> Let me tell you a story. When *The Grapes of Wrath* got loose, a lot of people were pretty mad at me. The undersheriff of Santa Clara County was a friend of mine and he told me

as follows—"Don't you go into any hotel room alone. Keep records of every minute and when you are off the ranch travel with one or two friends." "Why?" I asked. "Maybe I'm sticking my neck out but the boys got a rape case set up for you. You get alone in a hotel room and a dame will come in, tear off her clothes, scratch her face and scream and you try to talk yourself out of that one. They won't touch your book, but there's easier ways."

Twenty-two years later, "through a crude but mysterious alchemy," John Howard Griffin dyed his skin black and traveled through the vicious heart of the segregated south. His book *Black Like Me*, published in 1961, generated the same firestorm. Griffin was given the same warning as Steinbeck, virtually word-for-word.

Griffin eventually paid a harder price than Steinbeck for his searing honesty; 15 years after *Black Like Me* was published, Griffin traveled alone in the south (and let his guard down in doing so). The Klu Klux Klan found him one night in Mississippi, beat him with chains and left him for dead. He sustained permanent kidney damage, but he was not deterred. He continued to speak out against racial injustice ... and never mentioned the incident in any of his writings.

The Grapes of Wrath and *Black Like Me* became instant American classics (although not without their detractors); both have been printed in the millions of copies and widely translated around the world; both are still in print since their original publication dates, *The Grapes of Wrath*, 1939, and *Black Like Me*, 1961.

Chapter 25 of *The Grapes of Wrath* reveals his white hot anger, his moral vision—and indignation—of the injustices in California, of how crop prices were maintained and the surpluses dumped during those years:

> There is a crime here that goes beyond denunciation. There is a sorrow here that weeping cannot symbolize. There is a failure here that topples all our successes. The fertile earth, the straight tree rows, the sturdy trunks, and the ripe fruit. And children dying of pellagra must die because a profit cannot be taken from an orange. And coroners must fill in the certificates—died of malnutrition—because the food must rot, must be forced to rot.
>
> The people come with nets to fish for potatoes in the river, and the guards hold them back; they come in rattling cars to get the dumped oranges, but the kerosene is sprayed, and they stand still and watch the potatoes float by, listen to the screaming pigs being killed in a ditch and covered with quicklime, watch the mountains of oranges slop down to a putrefying ooze; and in the eyes of the people there is a growing wrath. In the souls of the people the grapes of wrath are filling and growing heavy, growing heavy for the vintage.

Today

Four |

Pre-Occupied:
The origins and future
of Occupy Wall Street

by Mattathias Schwartz
The New Yorker, Nov. 28, 2011

Kalle Lasn spends most nights shuffling clippings into
a binder of plastic sleeves, each of which represents one
page of an issue of *Adbusters*, a bimonthly magazine
that he founded and edits. It is tactile process, like making a collage, and occasionally Lasn will run a page with
his own looped cursive scrawl on it. From this absorbing work, Lasn acquired the habit of avoiding the news
after dark. So it was not until the morning of Tuesday,
November 15th, that he learned that hundreds of police
officers has massed in lower Manhattan at 1 a.m. and

cleared the camp at Zuccotti Park. If anyone claimed responsibility for the Zuccotti situation, it was Lasn: *Adbusters* had come up with the idea of an encampment, the date the initial occupation would start, and the name of the protest—Occupy Wall Street. Now the epicenter of the movement had been raided. Lasn began thinking of reasons that this might be a good thing.

Lasn is sixty-nine years old and lives with his wife on a five-acre farm outside Vancouver. He has thinning white hair and the small eyes of a bulldog. In a lilting voice, he speaks of "a dark age coming for humanity" and "killing capitalism," alternating gusts of passion with gentle laughter. He has learned not to let premonitions of apocalypse spoil his good mood.

The magazine, which he founded twenty-two years ago, depicts the developed world as a nightmare of environmental collapse and spiritual hollowness, driven to the brink of destruction by its consumer appetites. *Adbusters*' images—a breastfeeding baby tattooed with corporate logos, a smiling Barack Obama with a clowns' ball on his nose—are combined with equally provocative texts and turned into a paginated montage. *Adbusters* is not the only radical magazine calling for the end of life as we know it, but it is by far the best-looking.

Lasn was interrupted by a phone call about the Zuccotti eviction while in bed, reading Julian Barnes's "The Sense of an Ending." He rose and checked his e-mail. There was a message from Micah White, *Adbusters*' senior editor and Lasn's closest collaborator.

"Eerie timing!" White wrote. Earlier that night, *Adbusters* had sent out its most recent "tactical briefing"—a mass e-mail to ninety thousand friends of the magazine—proposing that the nation's Occupy protestors throw a party in mid-December, declare victory, and withdraw from their encampments. A few hours later, officers from the New York Police Department began handing out notices stating that the park had become dangerous and unsanitary, and ordering the protestors to leave, so that it could be cleaned. Those who refused to go were arrested, and whatever they left behind was carried off by the Department of Sanitation, to a depot on West Fifty-seventh street. After a long night of angry marches and meetings, the protestors were allowed back into Zuccotti, with newly enforced prohibitions on tents and on lying down. The protest continued, but the fifty-nine days of rude, anarchic freedom on a patch of granite in lower Manhattan were over.

White reaches Lasn by telephone shortly before nine. Lasn was in the bathtub, and White told him details that he learned online about the eviction. The police had established a strict media cordon, blocking access from nearby streets. "It was a military-style operation," he said. These words made Lasn think of the bloody uprising in Syria. He quickly decided that the apparent end of Zuccotti was not a tragedy but the latest in a series of crises-driven opportunities, what he calls "revolutionary moments," akin to the slapping of a Tunisian fruit vender. "I just can't believe how stupid Bloomberg can be!" he said to me later that day. "This means escalation. A raising of the stakes. It's one step closer to, you know, a revolution."

Lasn and white quickly hammered out a post-Zuccotti plan. White would draft a new memorandum, suggesting that Phase I—signs, meetings, camps, marches —- was now over. Phase II would involve a swarming strategy of "surprise attacks against business as usual," with the potential to be "more intense and visceral, depending on how the Bloombergs of the world react." White could hear the excitement in Lasn's voice. Even as Lasn vented about the morning's counterrevolution, he was doing what he could not to splash.

THIS IS HOW OCCUPY WALL Street began: as one of many half-formed plans circulating through conversations between Lasn and White, who lives in Berkeley and has not seen Lasn in person for more than four years. Neither can recall who first had the idea of trying to take over lower Manhattan. In early June, *Adbusters* sent an e-mail to subscribers stating that "American needs its own Tahrir.'" The next day, White wrote to Lasn that he was "very excited about the Occupy Wall Street meme.... I think we should make this happen." He proposed three possible Web sites: OccupyWallStreet.org, AcampadaWallStreet.org, and TakeWallStreet.org.

"No. 1 is best," Lasn replied, on June 9th. That evening he registered OccupyWallStreet.org.

White, who is twenty-nine years old, was born to a Caucasian mother and an African-American father. "I don't really fit into either group," he told me. He attended suburban public schools, where he began a series of one-man campaigns, against authority. In middle school, with his parents' blessing, he refused to stand for the Pledge of Allegiance. In high school, he founded an atheists' club over the objections of the principal. This led to an appearance on "Politically Incorrect," and atheist organizations flew White to their conferences to give talks. "It all went to my head," he said. "I became a little ego child. Ego destroys. I was too young to understand that."

Though he describes himself as a "mystical anarchist," White has three strict rules that govern his day: No naps. No snacks. Get dressed. "By dressed," he told me, "I mean pants and a shirt. Enough so if someone came to the door and knocked on it you wouldn't be totally embarrassed." After earning a B.A. at Swarthmore, he wrote a letter to Lasn, whom he had never met, saying that he would be arriving in Vancouver in a matter of weeks and wanted to be put to work.

Lasn was born in Estonia, but his earliest memories are of German refugee camps, where his family ended up after fleeing the Russian army during the Second World War. He remembers falling asleep on a cot as his uncles talked about politics with his father, a tennis champion who buried his trophies in the back yard before rushing the family onto one of the last boats to Germany. "World wars, revolutions — from time to time, big things actually happen," he told me. "When the moment is right, all it takes is a spark."

Lasn's family left the refugee camp for Australia, where he grew up. He has a degree in applied mathematics, and he began his career designing computer war games for the Australian military. Using this expertise, he started a market-research company in Tokyo, during Japan's post-war boom, where, by feeding punch cards into an I.B.M. mainframe, he created reports for consumer brands, many of them alcohol and tobacco products. "It's easy to generate cool if you have the bucks, the celebrities, the right ideas, the right slogans," he says. "You can throw ideas into the culture that then have a life of their own." He made a lot of money, travelled around the world, moved to Canada, and devoted himself to experimental filmmaking and environmental protection. In 1989, when the CBC refused to sell him airtime for a thirty-second "mind bomb" aimed at the forestry industry, Lasn realized that his politics would never have a place within the mass media. With Bill Schmalz, an outdoorsman who had worked with him as a cameraman, Lasn founded *Adbusters*.

Lasn says that *Adbusters* has a circulation world-wide of roughly seventy thousand. The magazine accepts no advertising, and relies on newsstand sales and donations. *Adbusters* was an early supporter of Buy Nothing Day, a protest holiday, in late November, during which people abstain from shopping. In 2003, Lasn started producing the Blackspot, a sneaker made partially of hemp, which he still sells online. Lasn has long used the magazine as a platform for stridently criticizing Israel's treatment of the Palestinians, and his most controversial moment came in 2004, when he wrote an essay on how Jews influence U.S. foreign policy. Alongside the essay was a list of powerful neo-conservatives with asterisks next to the names of those who Lasn believed were Jewish.

This spring, the magazine was pushing boycotts of Starbucks (for driving out local businesses) and the Huffington Post (for exploiting local journalists). Then, in early June, the art department designed a poster showing a ballerina poised on the "Charging Bull" sculpture, near Wall Street. Lasn had thought of the image late at night while walking his German shepherd Taka: "the juxtaposition of the capitalist dynamism of the bull," he remembers, "with the Zen stillness of the ballerina." In the background, protestors were emerging from a cloud of tear gas. The violence had a highly aestheticized, dreamlike quality—*Adbusters'* signature, "What is our demand?" the poster asked. "Occupy Wall Street. Bring tent."

White and Lasn spent a few days in early June debating when the occupation should start. At first, White argued that it should begin on July 4, 2012, so that protestors would have time to prepare. Lasn believed that the political climate could have shifted entirely by then. He proposed late September of this year; then he settled on the seventeenth, his mother's birthday. White agreed. Lasn instructed the art department to insert "September 17th" beneath the bull and the ballerina, and *Adbusters* devoted a tactical-briefing e-mail on July 13th exclusively to the proposed occupation.

White watched as the e-mail's proposal raced around Twitter and Reddit. "Normal campaigns are lots of drudgery and not much payoff, like rolling a snowball up a hill," he said. "This was the reverse." Fifteen minutes after Lasn sent the e-mail, Justine Tunney, a twenty-six-year-old in Philadelphia, read it on her RSS feed. The next day, she registered OccupyWallStreet.org, which soon became the movement's online headquarters. She began operating the site with a small team, most of whose members were, like her, transgender anarchists (They jokingly called themselves Trans World Order).

Encouraged by the quick online response, White connected with New Yorkers Against Budget Cuts, which had previously organized an occupation-style action, called Bloombergville, and was already planning an August 2nd rally at the "Charging Bull" to protest cuts that would likely result from the federal debt crisis. They agreed to join forces, and N.Y.A.B.C. said that it would devote part of its upcoming rally to planning for the September 17th occupation.

This resulted in some confusion on August 2nd, when scores of graduate students and labor activists showed up, expecting a rally for New Yorkers Against Budget Cuts. They erected a small stage and began giving amplified speeches, which alienated the roughly fifty *Adbusters* supporters, mostly anarchists, who came expecting a planning session. There was some angry shouting before a group of anarchists broke off, sat down in a circle on the cobblestones, and held their own meeting.

The anarchists immediately agreed to use "horizontal" organizing methods, according to which meetings are known as general assemblies and participants make decisions by consensus and give continuous feedback though hand gestures. Moving one's fingers in an undulating motion, palm out, pointing up, means approval of what's being said. Palm in, pointing down, means disapproval. Crossed arms signals a "block," a serious objection that must be heard. Some participants knew this style of meeting from left-wing traditions stretching back to the civil-rights movement and earlier.

Late that night, David Graeber, a fifty-year-old professor at the University of London and an anarchist theorist who helped facilitate the first meeting, sent an e-mail to White, in Berkeley, asking him for guidance. "How did it start?" Graeber asked. White told him, saying that the goal was "getting the meme out there, getting the people on the streets." he added, "We are not trying to control what happens."

Early on, Lasn and White said that the Wall Street occupiers needed a clear message. The revolutionaries in Cairo, they wrote, presented " a straight-forward ultimatum": they wouldn't leave the square until President Hosni Mubarak left office. *Adbusters* invited readers to "zero in on what our one demand will be." The suggested ideas included a Presidential commission charged with ending the influence of money in politics, and a one percent "Robin Hood tax" on all financial transactions.

After the August 2nd gathering, the movement's center of gravity shifted from Vancouver to New York. The protestors planning the September occupation met again, on August 9th, at the Irish Hunger Memorial, near Battery Park; all subsequent meetings were held on the south side of Tompkins Square Park. Early on, they decided to call the organization the New York City General Assembly.

In theory, the job of facilitating the meetings rotated among the eighty or so attendees. In practice, facilitation fell to a small smaller set of people who had experience with the general-assembly process. The leaderless movement was developing leaders. Graeber was among the first rank of equals, as was Marisa Holmes, a twenty-five-year-old anarchist and filmmaker. Holmes is dark-haired and eloquent; she has the parliamentarian's trick of making harsh ultimatums sound palatable, even breezy. When she wants to emphasize a point, she doesn't raise her voice; she turns her palms up and shrugs. Earlier this year, she flew to Cairo and filmed the Tahrir demonstrations. "They had speakers, banners, direct actions. I spent ninety percent of my time in cafes, drinking Turkish coffee and talking."

At 11 A.M. on Saturday, September 17th, an elementary-school teacher I'll call P. left his Brooklyn apartment and got on a subway heading to Manhattan. (He requested that he be identified by the first letter of his last name, because he was concerned that he would be fired from his job.) He wore a red sweater and brown pants. Earlier that morning, he sent a vague e-mail informing a co-worker that he might not show up Monday morning. He was part of the Tactical Committee, a subgroup of the General Assembly whose responsibility was to figure out where, exactly, the occupation would take place.

P. took the subway to Bowling Green. On his way to the exit, he passed a line of police officers accompanied by bomb-sniffing dogs. Outside, police had surrounded the "Charging Bull" with barricades and, a few blocks north, sealed off a stretch of Wall Street around the Stock Exchange. P. tried to look nonchalant as he carried a black messenger bag that contained a first-aid kit, a bottled solution of liquid antacid and water (to remedy the effects of tear gas and pepper spray), fifteen Clif bars (carrot cake), and several hundred photocopied maps, showing several possible locations. "We decided that low-tech communications would be best," P. told me. "If we'd used a mass text message, or

Twitter, it would have been easy for the police to track down who was doing this."

P. majored in math at a small liberal-arts college and plays in two bands, "some punk, some noise." Like most of Occupy Wall Street's core organizers, P. is an anarchist, meaning he is "dedicated to the eradication of any unjust or illegitimate system. At the very least, that means the eradication of capitalism and the state." He does not smash bank windows, though he said that he does not necessarily disapprove of those who do.

At Bowling Green several hundred protestors had gathered near the Museum of the American Indian. The previous week, members of the General Assembly had stocked up on food, made bail arrangements, and circulated flyers. Still, most of them had doubts that much would come of the occupation. "I, along with many others, expected that it would fizzle out in a couple of days," Marisa Holmes says.

P. quickly found the two other members of the Tactical Committee, both white men in their twenties. All three were "extremely nervous," P. says. They left to scout Location Two, three-quarters of an acre of honey-locust trees and granite benches, a few blocks to the north, called Zuccotti Park. It was almost empty, and there were few police nearby. As the Tactical Committee had learned in its research, Location Two was a privately owned public space. While the city can close public parks at dusk, or impose other curfews, zoning laws require Zuccotti's owner to keep the park open for "passive recreation" twenty-four hours a day.

Soon, maps were distributed and people began to murmur, "Go to Location Two in thirty minutes."

The first arrivals took seats beneath the trees on the eastern side, arranged themselves in small groups, and ate peanut-butter-and-jelly sandwiches. By that afternoon, nearly a thousand people had gathered for a general assembly meeting. Late that night, P. went home; nearly three hundred of his comrades settled into sleep there.

In the next few weeks, the encampment became more established, with tents, desks, walkways, wireless Internet, a kitchen, and an extensive lending library. A sort of organization took shape, with people forming a seemingly endless array of working groups: Structure, Facilitation, Sanitation, Food, Direct Action, Safe Spaces. A mid-October balance sheet from the occupation's Finance Working Group reported that it had received four hundred and fifty thousand dollars in donations, which it was keeping in two accounts at Amalgamated Bank. Almost every afternoon for two months, depending on the weather, hundreds of people gathered in the park. Some were drawn to the cameras and the spectacle; some came for the free food, shelter, and medical care; and some showed up for the earnest political conversation and because they believed that this might be the beginning of a revolution.

What did the movement want? On September 20th, three thousand miles way from Zuccotti Park, White and Lasn tried to write a manifesto in the form of a letter to President Obama. They sought to have banking-industry regulations tightened, high-frequency trading banned, all the "financial fraudsters" responsible for the 2008 crash arrested, and a Presidential commission formed to investigate corruption in politics. "We will stay here in our encampment in Liberty Plaza"—Zuccotti Park's post-occupation name—"until you respond to our demands," the letter concluded.

"Micah, this is a wonderful draft," Holmes replied on September 22nd, when White e-mailed her *Adbusters'* proposed letter. "However the General Assembly is going through this very process of drafting a statement. It should be ready this afternoon." A week later, the General Assembly adopted a "Declaration of the Occupation," which is more a world view than a list of demands. "We write so that all people who feel wronged by the corporate forces of the world can know that we are your allies.... No true democracy is attainable when the process is determined by economic power." The rest of the six-hundred word declaration is taken up mainly by "grievances," which place the blame for everything from poison in the food supply to cruelty to animals on those corporate forces, also known as "they." What should be done to remedy these grievances? "Exercise your right to peaceably assemble; occupy public space; create a process to address the problems we face; and generate solutions accessible to everyone."

To many in the park, vagueness was a virtue. It also had a history, In 1962, student radicals gathered in Michigan to complete the Port Huron Statement, the founding document of Students for a Democratic Society. One student argued that an early working draft was too utopian and impractical. But Tom Hayden, the main author wrote that the movement should "remain ambiguous in direction for a while: don't kill it by immediately imposing formulas.... When consciousness is at its proper stage, we might talk seriously and in an action-oriented way about solutions."

Soon after finishing the declaration, the early organizers started to have a problem: their solutions were to be accessible to everyone, but so was their protest. The crowds at those early meetings came in response to messages broadcast over a narrow channel, the *Adbusters* list. They were committed to a tangible goal, with an immediate deadline. But in early October, as the national media seized on the Zuccotti Park story, the rest of the ninety-nine percent started showing up. The G.A. had to tackle three new challenges simultaneously: holding ground; managing a semi-permanent village; and guiding a much larger and more cacophonous political conversation. All this had to be done with almost no heat, running water, or electricity.

Consensus—the agreed-upon method of decision-making—wasn't easy among hundreds of self-identified ninety-nine per-centers, whose politics ranged from "Daily Show" liberalism to insurrectionary anarchism. Because of the ground rules determined by the people sitting on the cobblestones in August, no decision could be made without giving everyone in attendance the chance to cross his or her arms and bring the meeting to a halt. According to the G.A.'s rules, a nine-tenths vote could override a block, but only after each block had explained his or her objections and the facilitators had responded. The least reasonable people often got the most time to speak.

"The G.A. is beautiful, but it's not an effective decision-making body," Homes told me in mid-October. She wanted things to be slightly more hierarchical, with a Spokes Council that would have limited day-to-day authority over the camp.

On October 28th, three dozen members of the Facilitation Working Group gathered around metal tables on a public atrium at 60 Wall Street to set that night's agenda. They were going to discuss Holmes's proposal again, but what else? An older man with bushy eyebrows was videotaping the proceedings. He said that he represented the Demands Working Group, and he wanted the G.A. to demand jobs for all. "The G.A. already said this is a movement without demands," another man said. "So how can there be a working group on demands?"

Other people approached the facilitators. A group of herbalists wanted fifteen hundred dollars to make medicines. Someone wanted to present "Native American peace principles" derived from the Iroquois Confederacy. Someone else had a facilitation accountability model, a spreadsheet for evaluating the facilitators. A representative from an N.Y.U. student group asked the G.A. to formally endorse Occupy Oakland's Day of Action. He was informed that such an endorsement had already been made. A few minutes later, everyone began speaking at once. "Whoa!" a facilitator cried. "Let's take a breath and get centered. This is a valid conversation, but this is not the right venue to have it."

As the facilitation meeting was wrapping up, Marisa Holmes, wearing a dark-green trenchcoat arrived: soon she was conferring with two other organizers over cold noodles about how they would present the proposal for the Spokes Council that evening. She had arrived with the team that was to conduct the general assembly, and the atrium quickly reorganized itself around them. Despite the movement's taboo on leaders, many in this group had accrued a sort of power. "Marisa is a quiet leader," Marina Sitrin, an occasional facilitator and the author of a book about horizontalism in Argentina. "She's not a young Tom Hayden, the white-male type who by force of personality and speech wins an argument."

When it was time for the general assembly, a crowd of four or five hundred had gathered around the steps on the park's east side. Most spent the next three hours packed in, knee to knee, on the cold stone. "I hope everyone's doing well!" Nelini Stamp, one of the facilitators, cried. "High hopes! High energy!"

"This is going to take forever," someone in front muttered.

Stamp ignored him. she began leading the general assembly in the song "Solidarity Forever."

"Not everyone here is into your narrow union politics," the voice in front said.

"It's not a union song," Stamp said, "It's union like 'unity.'"

The voice came from a man in his mid-twenties wearing a camouflage jacket. He was sitting on a concrete bench in front of the facilitation team, one boot resting on his knee, eating sweet-potato chips and drinking from a Starbucks cup. He had the haggard look of someone who had spent a few weeks sleeping outside in a city. Known to other occupiers as Sage, he had written "SAGES" on the brim of his baseball cap in marker. Sage continued speaking as Holmes presented the proposal. "These are all tourists," he said. "You do not live here." Every time he spoke, the people sitting next to him stiffened and frowned. Sage did not seem to notice.

During a twenty-minute breakout session to discuss the proposal, Lisa Fithian, a fifty-year-old organizer who works with Holmes, made her way to the bench in front and told Sage about her success with the Spokes Council model. She said she had worked on the nineteen-seventies anti-nuclear campaign and the W.T.O. protests in Seattle, in 1999.

"This is not a fucking college dorm," Sage said. "Until you can speak honestly with me, I'm not having a conversation."

"Shut the fuck up," Fithian said. "I don't need this shit in my face."

"Look, I was at Tompkins Square Park," Sage said. "This whole thing has been hijacked by socialist students who have insinuated themselves into the square. These people don't see me. They don't think I comprehend. So I see everything."

"I hear you," Fithian said.

"Why should someone who lives here have to conform to a bunch of tourists?" Sage asked.

"Your energy is hurting my system," Fithian replied.

"Look, sometimes you have to put your body on the machine," Sage said.

"This is not the machine!" Fithian said, her voice rising.

A tall man with a stubbled face tried to calm Sage down. His name as Evan Wagner and he was wearing a red North Face jacket. Like Sage, he was one of the few people sleeping in the park who bothered with general assemblies. Unlike Sage, he seemed like someone who could find a job if he wanted one.

Sage waved Wagner off. "Dude, you are playing a homeless person," he said. Soon Sage was quiet. It was though Fithian had absorbed Sage's rage so the rest of the meeting would not have to.

When everyone returned, each smaller group described its concerns about the Spokes Council proposal. There was a question about exactly how blocks would work, and worries about a "Spokes Council-ocracy." The tall office buildings were funnelling a cold breeze in from the Hudson River. Around ten, a facilitator called for a vote. "Three hundred people are frustrated," she said. "Hundreds are getting frustrated. All of those in favor, please raise one hand." Sage raised his hand.

The facilitation team counted the votes and added them up on a cellphone. The proposal passed, two hundred and eighty-four to seventeen. Stamp jumped up and down. Her voice was hoarse from three hours of yelling. "Everyone is beautiful!" she shouted. "Everyone is awesome!"

Those who were around at the beginning of the Occupy Wall Street movement talk about the old "vertical" left versus the new "horizontal" one. By "vertical," they mean hierarchy and its trappings—leaders, demands, and issue-specific rallies. They mean social change as laid out by Saul Alinsky's "Rules for Radicals" and Barack Obama's "Dreams from My Father," where outside organizations spur communities to action. "Horizontal" means leaderless—like the 1999 W.T.O. protests in Seattle, the Arab Spring and even the Tea Party. Anyone can show up at a general assembly and claim a piece of the movement. This lets people feel important immediately, and gives them implicit permission to take action. It also gives a disproportionate amount of power to people like Sage.

One influence that is often cited by the movement is open-source software, such as Linux, which competes with Microsoft Windows and Apple's OS but doesn't have an owner or a chief engineer. A programmer named Linus Torvalds came up with the idea. Thousands of unpaid amateurs joined him and then eventually organized into work groups. Some coders have more influence than others, but anyone can modify the software and no one can sell it. According to Justine Tunney, who continues to help run OccupyWallStreet.org, "There is leadership in the sense of deference, just as people defer to Linus Torvalds. But the moment people stop respecting Torvalds, they can fork it"—meaning copy what's been built and use it to build something else.

In mid-October, supporters in Tokyo, Sydney, Madrid, and London held rallies; encampments sprang up in almost every major American city. Nearly all of them modelled themselves on the New York City General Assembly: with no official leaders, rotating facilitators, and no fixed set of demands. Today, endorsements of the Occupy movement can be found everywhere, from anarchist graffiti on bank walls to Al Gore's Twitter feed. On a rain-smeared cardboard sign near the shattered window of an Oakland coffee shop that had been destroyed by a cadre of anarchists during a nighttime clash with police, someone wrote, "We're sorry, but this does not represent us." Below that, someone else wrote, "Speak for yourself."

At times, horizontalism can feel like utopian theatre. Its greatest invention is the "people's mike," which starts when someone shouts, "Mike check!" Then the crowd shouts "Mike check!" and the phrases (phrases!) are transmitted (are transmitted!) through mass chanting (through mass chanting!). In the same way that poker ritualizes capitalism and North Korea's mass games ritualize totalitarianism, the people's mike ritualizes horizontalism. The problem, though, comes when multiple people try to summon the mike simultaneously. Then it can feel a lot like anarchy.

The politics of the occupation run parallel to the mainstream left—the people's mike was used to shout down Michelle Bachmann and Governor Scott Walker, of Wisconsin, in early November. But, in the end, the point of Occupy Wall Street is not its platform so much as its form: people sit down and hash things out instead of passing their complaints on to Washington. "We are our demands," as the slogan goes, and horizontalism seems made for this moment. It relies on people forming loose connections quickly—something that modern technology excels at.

Events in New York seemed to bear out Lasn's hunch that the temporary evection of the protestors from Zuccotti Park was an opportunity rather than a defeat. The organizers were quickly able to regroup and agree that they should return to the park, despite the newly enforced ban on tents. Last Thursday, the movement mounted one of the largest protests to date. Demonstrators tried to shut down the New York Stock Exchange (they failed), organized a sit-in at the base of the Brooklyn Bridge, and tussled with police in Zuccotti Park. More than two hundred people were arrested. Similar Day of Action protests temporarily blocked bridges in Chicago, St. Louis, Detroit, Houston, Milwaukee, Portland and Philadelphia.

No matter what happens next, the movement's center is likely to shift from the N.Y.C.G.A., just as it shifted from *Adbusters*, and form somewhere else, around some other circle of people, ideas and plans. "This could be the greatest thing that I work on in my life," Justine Tunney, of OccupyWallStreet.org said. "But the movement will have other Web sites. Over the coming weeks and months, as other occupations become more prominent, ours will slowly become irrelevant." She sounded as though the irrelevance of her project were both inevitable and desirable. "We can't hold on to any of that authority," she continued. "We don't want to."

After the phone call with White, on the morning the New York police cleared Zuccotti Park, Lasn drove to Vancouver, to a hundred-year-old house that serves as *Adbusters'* headquarters. Lasn rents the top two floors, which look down on Granville Island and False Creek; he runs the magazine out of the basement.

Lasn flung down his battered briefcase in the cramped conference room that he uses as an office. There is a phone, but no computer, and Lasn spent most of the day sitting at a table and brainstorming with his employees, the oldest of whom was thirty-two. After conferring with an *Adbusters* writer and the office manager, he modified that morning's bathtub plan. The next tactical briefing would be split up into a series of e-mails sent out over time. "The chessboard has been overturned, and now a new game begins!" Lasn reasoned, shortly after noon. "The stakes are so much higher this time. First, we need to let the dust settle."

Lasn called White to talk about this new plan, but White had already left for the University of California's Doe Library, where he spends his afternoons looking for snippets of radical thought for Lasn's plastic sleeves. It's the point in his day when he leaves behind all electronic devices to seek what he calls "a burst of clarity."

White is not on Facebook, which he calls "the commercialization of friendship." He uses e-mail and Twitter only because he feels compelled to. His position has softened since the time when he believed in what he calls "the Heideggerian critique of technology—that it turns us into empty matter for the exportation of capitalism." Lasn welcomes the international media attention that *Adbusters* has received. "I'm surfing," he said, when I asked if he ever felt swamped by the flood of incoming messages. White feels differently: "All those e-mails—it feels like a denial-of-service attack against my brain."

Every day, as White walks from his home to the library, he is confronted by traces of what he helped create: posters in store windows supporting a general strike in Oakland; posters supporting the occupation wheat-pasted onto a football statue; "We are the 99 Percent!" slogans written on walls in chalk.

"I almost feel like I'm a ghost, or like I'm living in a dream, where my conversations with Kalle have manifested in reality," he said. In mid-November, sixteen hours after someone created a short "Micah M. White" entry on Wikipedia, White nominated it for deletion. "Person is non-notable," he wrote.

Five |

Occupy Wall Street timeline

July 13, 2011:

Adbusters publishes a blogpost asking for people to rally on Wall Street.

The important point they make is that there should be no official leadership at the protests, and that what the group hopes to achieve may only be decided when the entire group agrees. The movement was spearheaded by a group and was meant to be carried out by a group.

The hashtag #occupywallstreet first shows up on Twitter.

July 26:

A website, Facebookpage, and Twitter profile have been created for the movement by this time.

Adbusters asks for global involvement after less than two weeks of domestic protests.

August 23:

The hacktivists at Anonymous debut a video to show their support for Occupy Wall Street.

They also promote OWS on Twitter.

September 17 (Day 1 of the Occupy Movement):

Rally and march day. Occupy Wall Street sets up a temporary city in Zuccotti Park, New York City.

OWS's city has its own newspaper, food and wi-fi.

Police and protestors begin to clash.

September 19:

Keith Olbermann, of Current TV, becomes the first major journalist to focus on the protests. A couple of days later, Olbermann criticizes mainstream media for failing to covert Occupy Wall Street, saying "Why isn't any major news outlet covering this? ... If that's a Tea Party protest in front of Wall Street ... , it's the lead story on every network newscast."

September 20:

Police arrest mask-wearing protestors, using a law dating back to 1845 which bans masked gatherings unless part of a "masquerade party or like entertainment."

September 24:

Over 80 people are arrested during an NYC march to Union Square. Accusations fly against the NYPD when its use of excessive force and pepper spray is brought under fire.

October 1:

Over 700 people are arrested while marching across the Brooklyn Bridge.

NYPD says the myriad protestors were blocking traffic.

October 5:

Nearly three months after the movement's inception, major unions across the United States begin to support the protests.

In fact, Occupy Wall Street's approval rating was 19 points higher than that of Congress that day—33 percent approval to Congress' 14 percent.

October 6:

An estimated 5,000 to 15,000 demonstrators march from lower Manhattan's Foley square to Zuccotti Park. The movement begins to spread much faster across the United States.

In the nation's capital of Washington, D.C., protestors vow they will occupy the city for weeks.

October 11:

As must be expected with every movement, a counter-movement develops.

"The 53 %," a play on the 99 percent that Occupy protestors identify with, claims to be the percentage of the working class that pays to support the protestors.

"The 53 %" feel the protestors are complaing publicly to avoid working, thereby missing out on perhaps attaining a higher financial class.

October 12:

NYC Mayor Michael Bloomberg tells the protestors they must vacate so that Zuccotti Park can be cleaned. Not to be discouraged, the protestors begin cleaning the park themselves.

October 14:

In response to a job well-done, Zuccotti Park's property management company, Brookfield Properties, decides that the protestors do not have to vacate the park for cleaning.

October 15:

Occupy Wall Street has occupied Earth. 951 cities in 82 countries hold protests. Thousands of protestors marched through Manhattan to Times Square where they faced a U.S. Armed Forces recruiting station to protest the money being spent on foreign wars instead of on people in the U.S. struggling with no jobs and no healthcare. Cornel West was arrested on the steps of the Supreme Court in Washington, D.C., protesting corporate influence in politics.

October 17:

Adbusters side with Robin Hood, asking for a global Robin Hood March at G20, on October 29.

The march would promote a Robin Hood tax on the 1 percent—take from the rich, give to the poor.

October 19:

The NYPD announces plans of discipline for an officer who pepper-sprayed women on September 24.

October 25:

500 protestors in Oakland refuse orders to move. The police respond with tear gas to clear them out.

October 26:

Since the number of shooting victims in NYC in the first week of October was 154 percent higher than the same time in 2010, NYPD blames Occupy Wall Street on the rise in gun crime.

The number was up 28 percent for the entire month.

Digital takeover:

Occupy Wall Street is in 82 countries, 951 cities worldwide.

Its Facebook page has over 100,000 fans.

There are over 14,000 followers on Twitter.

Meet-Up has formed 2,340 groups worldwide for local protests.

On October 27, 2011, #occupywallstreet was tweeted 918.4 times per hour.

Beliefs:

80 percent of surveyed protestors believe the very rich should pay higher taxes.

88 percent believe the government should limit the salaries of CEOs.

98 percent think health care should be free, and the same amount believe insurance companies profit too much.

95 percent believe the government should regulate prescription drugs prices.

32.5 percent believe the government would manage health care poorly.

93 percent feel student loans should be forgiving, and also that internet and cell phones should be free.

How much of the national wealth is consumed by the 1 percent?

In the United states, the top 1 percent earns 20 percent of national wealth.

In the United Kingdom, they earn 16 percent.

In Canada, 14 percent of national wealth is earned by the top earners.

In Germany, Belgium, Portugal, Australia and Japan, the top 1 percent earns about 10 percent of the national wealth.

Poverty:

5 percent of United States citizens live in poverty.

That number is 9 percent in Canada.

10 percent of Australians live below the poverty line.

14 percent of United Kingdom residents live in poverty.

In Belgium it's 15 percent.

In Germany and Japan, 16 percent.

Portugal is home to 18 percent of citizens living in poverty.

It's worth noting, however, that some protestors in the "the 99 percent" make about a half million dollars annually.

Slogans:

Aside from the "We are the 99%" slogan that Occupy Wall Street is known for, there are some other popular slogans seen on signs globally.

These include "We Are Too Big to Fail," "Will Work for Money," "Human Need Not Corporate Greed," "OUT$OURCED," and "People Over Profits."

November 17:

More than 30,000 marched in the streets of New York. Crowds assembled around Zuccotti Park, Union Square, Foley Square, the Brooklyn Bridge and other locations throughout the city.

November 19:

Former Philadelphia Police Captain Ray Lewis was arrested at Zuccotti Park. Protestors at the University of California, Davis, were pepper sprayed, promoting outrage. Newt Gingrich, former Speaker of the House suggests protestors "Go get a job right after you take a bath."

November 23:

While giving a speech in New Hampshire, President Obama was interrupted by "The Peoples Mic" by Occupy Wall Street protestors. They said "Mr. President, over four thousand peaceful protestors have been arrested."

November 30:

Police enter the Occupy Los Angeles Wall Street encampment at City Hall and arrest protestors defying an eviction notice.

January 2, 2012:

Occupy protestors interrupted Republican Presidential candidate Mitt Romney's speech in Des Moines, Iowa, by shouting at the candidate.

January 10:

Hundreds of Occupy Wall Street protestors reentered Zuccotti Park after the barricades surrounding the park were removed. NYPD is enforcing new rules set by the owner that protestors are not allowed to lay down or sleep in the park.

January 17:

Over 2,000 people attended a protest on the West Lawn of the Capital Building for an event called Occupy Congress.

January 25:

Recalling the 1968 Chicago protests, *Adbusters*, the magazine which has been credited with launching the Occupy movement, publishes an ad calling for 50,000 protestors to Occupy the G8 summit scheduled for May, 2012.

Six |

Declaration of the Occupation of New York City

THIS DOCUMENT WAS ACCEPTED by the NYC General Assembly on September 29, 2011. Translations: French, Slovak, Spanish, German, Italian, Arabic, Portuguese.

As we gather together in solidarity to express a feeling of mass injustice, we must not lose sight of what brought us together. We write so that all people who feel wronged by the corporate forces of the world can know that we are your allies.

As one people, united, we acknowledge the reality: that the future of the human race requires the cooperation of its members; that our system must protect our rights, and upon corruption of that system, it is up to the individuals to protect their own rights, and those of their neighbors, that a democratic government derives its just power from the people, but corporations do not seek consent to extract wealth from the people and the Earth; and that no true democracy is attainable when the process is determined by economic power. We come to you at a time when corporations, which place profit over people, self-interest over justice, and oppression of equality, run our government. We have peaceably assembled here, as is our right, to let these facts be known.

>
They have taken our houses through an illegal foreclosure process, despite not having the original mortgage.

They have taken bailouts from taxpayers with impunity, and continue to give Executives exorbitant bonuses.

They have perpetuated inequality and discrimination in the workplace based on age, the color of one's skin, sex, gender identity and sexual orientation.

They have poisoned the food supply through negligence, and undermined the faming system through monopolization.

They have profited off the torture, confinement and cruel treatment of countless animals, and actively hide these practices.

They have continuously sought to strip employees of the right to negotiate for better pay and safer working conditions.

They have held students hostage with tens of thousands of dollars of debt on education, which it itself a human right.

They have continuously outsourced labor and used that outsourcing as leverage to cut workers' healthcare and pay.

They have influenced the courts to achieve the same rights as people, with none of the culpability or responsibility.

They have spent millions of dollars on legal teams that look for ways to get them out of contracts in regards to health insurance.

They have sold our privacy as a commodity.

They have used the military and police force to prevent freedom of the press.

They have deliberately declined to recall faulty products endangering lives in pursuit of profit.

They determine economic policy, despite the catastrophic failures that their policies have produced and continue to produce.

They have donated large sums of money to politicians, who are responsible for regulating them.

They continue to block alternative forms of energy to keep us dependent on oil.

They continue to block generic forms of medicine that could save people's lives or provide relief in order to protect investments that have already turned a substantial profit.

They have purposely covered up oil spills, accidents, faulty bookkeeping, and inactive ingredients in pursuit of profit.

They purposefully keep people misinformed and fearful through the control of the media.

They have accepted private contracts to murder prisoners even when presented with serious doubts about their guilt.

They have perpetuated colonialism at home and abroad.

They have participated in the torture and murder of innocent civilians overseas.

They continue to create weapons of mass destruction in order to receive government contracts.

(These grievances are not all-inclusive.)

To the people of the world,

We, the New York General Assembly occupying Wall Street in Liberty Square, urge you to assert your power.

Exercise your right to peaceably assemble: occupy public space; create a process to address the problems we face, and generate solutions accessible to everyone.

To all communities that take action and form groups in the spirit of direct democracy, we offer support, documentation, and all of the resources at our disposal.

Join us and make your voices heard!

Seven |

U.S. Poverty: Census finds nearly half of Americans are poor or low-income

The Huffington Post, December 15, 2011

WASHINGTON—Squeezed by rising living costs, a record number of Americans—nearly 1 in 2—have fallen into poverty or are scraping by on earnings that classify them as low income.

The latest census data depict a middle class that's shrinking as unemployment stays high and the government's safety net frays. The new numbers follow years of stagnating wages for the middle class that have hurt millions of workers and families.

"Safety net programs such as food stamps and tax credits kept poverty from rising even higher in 2010, but for many low-income families with work-related and medical expenses. They are considered too 'rich' to qualify," said Sheldon Danziger, a University of Michigan public policy professor who specializes in poverty.

"The reality is that prospects for the poor and the near poor are dismal," he said. "If Congress and the states make further cuts, we can expect the number of poor and low-income families to rise for the next several years."

Congressional Republicans and Democrats are sparring over legislation that would renew a Social Security payroll tax cut, part of a year-end political showdown over economic priorities that could also trim unemployment benefits, freeze federal pay and reduce entitlement spending.

Robert Rector, a senior research fellow at the conservative Heritage Foundation, questioned whether some people classified as poor or low-income actually suffer material hardship. He said that while safety-net programs have helped many Americans, they have gone too far, citing poor people who live in decent-size houses, drive cars and own wide-screen TVs.

"There's no doubt the recession has thrown a lot of people out of work and incomes have fallen," Rector said. "As we come out of recession, it will be important that these programs promote self-sufficiency rather than dependence and encourage people to look for work."

Mayors in 29 cities say more than 1 in 4 people needing emergency food assistance did not receive it.

Many middle-class Americans are dropping below the low-income threshold—roughly $45,000. for a family of four—because of pay cuts, a forced reduction of work hours or a spouse losing a job. Housing and child-care costs are consuming up to half of a family's income.

States in the South and West had the highest shares of low-income families, including Arizona, New Mexico, and South Carolina, which have scaled back or eliminated aid programs for the needy. By raw numbers, such families were most numerous in California and Texas, each with more than 1 million.

The struggling Americans include Zenobia Bechtol, 18, in Austin, Texas, who earns minimum wage as a part-time pizza delivery driver. Bechtol and her 7-month-old baby were recently evicted from their bed-bug-infested apartment after her boyfriend, an electrician, lost his job in the sluggish economy.

After an 18-month job search, Bechtol's boyfriend now works as a waiter and the family of three is temporarily living with her mother.

"We're paying my mom $200 a month for rent, and after diapers and formula and gas for work, we barely have enough money to spend," said Bechtol, a high school graduate who wants to go to college. "If it weren't for food stamps and other government money for families who need help, we wouldn't be able to survive."

About 97.3 million Americans fall into a low-income category, commonly defined as those earning between 100 and 199 percent of the poverty level, based on a new supplemental measure by the Census Bureau that is designed to provide a fuller picture of poverty. Together with the 49.1 million who fall below the poverty level and are counted as poor, they number 146.4 million, or 48 percent of the U.S. population. That's up by 4 million from 2009, the earliest numbers for the newly developed poverty measure.

, The new measure of poverty takes into account medical, commuting and other living costs. Doing that helped push the number of people below 200 percent of the poverty level up from 104 million, or 1 in 3 Americans, that was officially reported in September.

Broken down by age, children were the most likely to be poor or low-income—about 57 percent—followed by seniors over 65. By race and ethnicity, Hispanics topped the list at 73 percent, followed by blacks, Asians and non-Hispanic whites.

Even by traditional measures, many working families are hurting.

Following the recession that began in late 2007, the share of working families who are low income has risen for three straight years to 31.2 percent, or 10.2 million. That proportion is the highest in at least a decade, up from 27 percent in 2002, according to a new analysis by the Working Poor Families Project and the Population Reference Bureau, a non-profit research group based in Washington.

Among the low-income families, about one-third were considered poor while the remainder—6.9 million—earned income just above the poverty line. Many states phase out eligibility for food stamps, Medicaid, tax credit and other government aid programs for low-income Americans as they approach 200 percent of the poverty level.

The majority of low-income families—62 percent—spent more than one-third of their earnings on housing, surpassing a common guideline for that is considered affordable. By some census surveys, child-care costs consume close to another one-fifth.

Paychecks for low-income families are shrinking. The inflation-adjusted average earnings for the bottom 20 percent of families have fallen from $16,788 in 1989 to just under $15,000, and earnings for the next 20 percent have remained flat at $37,000. In contrast, higher-income brackets had significant wage growth since 1979, with earnings for the top 5 percent of families climbing 64 percent to more than $313,000.

A survey of 29 cities conducted by the U.S. Conference of Mayors released Thursday points to a gloomy outlook for those on the lower end of the income scale.

Many mayors cited the challenges of meeting increased demands for food assistance, expressing particular concern about possible cuts to federal programs such as food stamps and WIC, which assists low-income pregnant women and mothers. Unemployment led the list of causes of hunger in cities, followed by poverty, low wages and high housing costs.

Among the 29 cities, about 27 percent of the people needing emergency food aid did not receive it. Kansas City, Mo., Nashville, Tenn., Sacramento, Calif., and Trenton, N.J., were among the cities that pointed to increases in the cost of food and declining food donations, while Mayor Michael McGinn in Seattle citied an unexpected spike in food requests from immigrants and refugees, particularly from Somalia, Burma and Bhutan.

Among those requesting emergency food assistance, 51 percent were in families, 26 percent were employed, 19 percent were elderly and 11 percent were homeless.

"People who never thought they would need food are in need of help," said Mayor Sly James of Kansas City, Mo., who co-chairs a mayors' task force on hunger and homelessness.

Eight

Report: Child homelessness up 33 percent in 3 years

ONE IN 45 CHILDREN in the USA—1.6 million children— were living on the street, in homeless shelters or motels, or doubled up with other families last year, according to the National Center on Family Homelessness.

The numbers represent a 33 percent increase from 2007, when there were 1.2 million homeless children, according to a report the center is releasing Tuesday.

"This is an absurdly high number," says Ellen Bassuk, president of the center. "What we have new in 2010 is the effects of a man-made disaster caused by the economic recession.... We are seeing extreme budget cuts, foreclosures and a lack of affordable housing," Marisol Bello wrote in *USA Today*, Dec. 13, 2011.`

The summary of the most recent report by The National Center on Family Homelessness includes the following:

> 1.6 million America children, or one in 45 children, are homeless in a year.
>
> This equates to more than 30,000 children each week, and more than 4,400 per day.
>
> Children experiencing homeless suffer from hunger, poor physical and emotional health, and missed educational opportunities.
>
> A majority of these children have limited educational proficiency in math and reading.
>
> Not surprisingly, the risks for homelessness—such as extreme poverty and worst case housing needs—have worsened with the economic recession, even though the total housing capacity for families increased by more than 15,000 units in the past four years, primarily due to the federal Homeless Prevention and Rapid Re-Housing Program (HPRP).
>
> Despite this bleak picture, planning and policy activities to support the growth and development of these vulnerable children remain limited. Sixteen states have done no planning related to child homelessness and only seven states have extensive plans.

Although the majority of homeless children reside in a few states (50 percent reside in six states, 75 percent reside in 18 states), thousands and tens of thousands of children in every state go to sleep each night without home to call their own. The numbers of homeless children in 2010 are likely undercounted, since data collection procedures changed in California, reducing California's reported total by 162,822 children in a single year, from 2009 to 2010. In the three previous data years (2007, 2008 and 2009), California accounted for more than 25 percent of the nation's homeless children.

America's Youngest Outcasts 2010 also analyzes trends in child homelessness since the publication of our first Report Card:

2006: A Natural Disaster Strikes—
Hurricanes Katrina and Rita

1.5 million American children, more than one in 450 children, go to sleep without homes to call their own in 2006.

A significant spike in child homelessness occurs due to 2005 Hurricanes Katrina and Rita, a historic natural disaster. The storms lead to one of the greatest mass migrations in our nation's history, accounting for the large numbers of homeless children in 2006.

2007: Recovery from the Hurricanes—
Child Homeless Drops by 25 Percent

1.2 million American children, or one in 63 children are homeless in 1997.

The numbers of children experiencing homelessness decrease dramatically as families resettle after the two hurricanes. There are more than 385,000 fewer homeless children in 2007 from 2006, a reduction of 25 percent.

In the six states most impacted by Katrina and Rita, the numbers of homeless children decrease by more than 450,000 (Mississippi was an exception, with their numbers slightly increasing.)

2007–2010: A Man-Made Disaster Strikes, Pushing Child Homeless Up by 38 Percent

Financial speculation sparks collapse of the housing market and financial institutions, a stock market crash and the Great Recession. The numbers of homeless children increase by more than 448,000 from 2007 to 2010. 1.6 million (one in 45 children) are homeless in 2010—that is a 38 percent spike from 2007.

Only five states report decreases in the numbers of homeless children from 2007 to 2010.

Fallout from the man-made disaster is worse than the natural disaster; driving the national total of homeless children above the hurricane year (2006) by more than 60,000 children.

All states are adversely affected by the economic downturn; changes in the structural determinants that contribute to the risk of homelessness vary by state.

In addition to documenting the extent of child homelessness, the well-being of homeless children risk factors for child homelessness, and policy responses, *America's Youngest Outcasts 2010* offers solutions to this national tragedy. Mindful of the severe constraints that our struggling economy is placing on institutions and individuals, we recommend affordable policy strategies in the areas of housing, child care, education, domestic violence, and employment that will help stabilize children and families who are homeless or at imminent risk of homelessness. We also urge that programs addressing and preventing child and family homelessness not be cut further.

America's Youngest Outcasts 2010 is a call to action for all of us to address child homelessness before we lose another generation. Please join us in demanding a rapid response now so our next Report card can paint a brighter picture of our nation's most vulnerable children.

Background

Children experiencing homeless are America's Youngest Outcasts. They have gradually become a prominent part of a Third World that is emerging within our own nation. Despite their growing numbers, homeless children are invisible to most of us; they have no voice and no constituency. Without a bed to call their own, these children have lost safety, privacy, and the comforts of home as well as their friends, possessions, pets, reassuring routines, and communities. Their losses combine to create a life-altering experience that inflicts profound and lasting scars.

America's Youngest Outcasts: The First Report card

Committed to ensuring that not one child is homeless for even one day, The National Center on Family Homelessness (The National Center) gave them a voice by creating *America's Youngest Outcasts: State Report Card on Child Homelessness*. The report presented vital information about the needs of these extremely vulnerable children and their families for the first time in a single document—including state-by-state data on (1) extent of the problem, (2) well-being of the children (3) risks for child homelessness (e.g., structural determinants), and (4) the policy response. Each state was ranked in those four domains and an overall rank was computed based on a composite of the domains.

Based on data reported in 2006 by Local Education Agencies (LEAs), as mandated by the federal McKinney-Vento Homeless Assistance Act, the first Report Card documented that 1.5 million, or more than one in 50, of our nation's children go to sleep without a home each year (The National Center on Family Homelessness 2009). We used this data source because schools are the only institution nationally that is legally responsible for identifying and serving homeless children.

The first Report Card described the well-being of children experiencing homelessness and found that many frequently go hungry, not knowing where their next meal will come from. Not surprisingly, these children had disproportionately high rates of chronic health conditions, asthma, traumatic stress, and emotional problems compared to their housed counterparts. Their educational proficiency in math and reading was extremely limited. To further understand why families and children are homeless in a country as affluent as ours, we created a risk index that focused on the structural determinants of family homelessness. We included indicators of poverty, household structure, housing market factors, and generosity of benefits—all at the state level.

Most importantly, we found that despite the severity of the problem, state level planning and policy responses were very limited. Few states in our first Report Card had developed strategies for combating child homelessness, although many had developed 10-Year Plans to prevent and end homelessness generally. Only six states had done extensive planning focused on ending child and family homelessness. After publishing the first Report Card, we launched a national Campaign to End Child Homelessness (see www.HomelessChildrenAmerica.org).

Definition of Homelessness

This Report Card describes homeless children from birth to age 18 who are accompanied by one or more parents or caregivers; by definition, they comprise a homeless family. Our counts and descriptions do not include unaccompanied children and youth (e.g., runaway, throw away, or homeless youth). The Report Card uses the definition of homelessness contained in

Subtitle B of Title VII of the McKinney-Vento Homeless Assistance act, Title X, of the No Child Left Behind Act of 2001 and adopted by the U.S. Department of Education. The definition includes children and youth who are:

Sharing the housing of other persons due to loss of housing, economic hardship, or a similar reason;

Living in motels, hotels, trailer parks or camping grounds due to the lack of alternative accommodations;

Living in emergency or transitional shelters;

Abandoned in hospitals;

Awaiting foster care placement;

Using a primary nighttime residence that is a public or private place not designed for, or ordinarily used as, a regular sleeping accommodation for human beings;

Living in cars, parks, public spaces, abandoned buildings, substandard housing, bus or train stations, or similar settings; and

Migratory children who qualify as homeless because they are living in circumstances described above.

Nine

Banks may have illegally foreclosed on nearly 5,000 military members

The Huffington Post, November 29, 2011

EVEN THOSE PEOPLE putting their lives on the line for their country may not be safe from the American foreclosure crisis.

Ten lenders are reviewing close to 5,000 foreclosures of homes belonging to active-duty service members in an attempt to discover if there were carried out improperly, according to data from the Office of the Comptroller of the Currency, cited by the *Financial Times*. The OCC's report is based on projections prepared by the bankers and their consultants. Bank of American said it is reviewing 2,400 foreclosures of homes belonging to active-duty service members and Wells Fargo said it's looking at nearly 900 cases. Citigroup is reviewing 700 foreclosures, the bank said.

The Servicemembers Civil Relief Act aims to protect active-duty members of the military from financial difficulty, including through measures that restrict foreclosures on properties owned by active-duty military members. Still, as the OCC data indicates, thousands of active-duty members of the armed forces have lost their homes while fighting abroad.

Bank of America and Morgan Stanley reached deals with the Justice Department earlier this year, agreeing to pay more than $20 million to settle claims that they foreclosed on more than 175 active-duty service members without court orders.

They're not the only ones. JPMorganChase also admitted to illegally foreclosing on the families of 27 active-duty military members earlier this year and has very publicly attempted to give the families back their homes or compensate them for damages if the house was sold.

The bank also agreed to pay $27 million in cash to about 6,000 active-duty service members who were overcharged on their mortgages, Bloomberg reports.

Illegal foreclosures have affected service members like U.S. Army Sgt. James Hurley who lost his house to foreclosure while he was serving in Iraq. Tim Collette said in June that he had been negotiating with JPMorganChase since 2008 to save his house from foreclosure while his son was fighting in Iraq.

Ten

Study: U.S. income inequality higher than Roman Empire levels

by Jillian Berman
The Huffington Post, December 19, 2011

MANY TOUT THE U.S. as the Roman Empire of the modern world. But as it turns out, that comparison may not be all good.

Income inequality in America is at levels even higher than those in ancient Rome, according to a recent study from two historians, Walter Schiedel and Steven Friesen, cited by Per Square Mile. After analyzing papyri ledgers, biblical passages and other previous scholarly estimates, the researchers found that the top one percent of earners in Ancient Rome controlled 16 percent of the society's wealth. By comparison, the top one percent of American earners control 40 percent of the country's wealth, according to *Vanity Fair*.

These findings add to the growing chorus of studies and criticism indicating the wealth gap is hitting truly remarkable levels. The top one percent saw their incomes rise by 275 percent between 1979 and 2007, according to the Congressional Budget Office, while the bottom fifth of earners only saw their incomes grow by 20 percent during the same period.

In addition, the total net worth of the bottom 60 percent is less than that of the Forbes 400 richest Americans.

Perhaps even more shocking, the six heirs to the retail giant Walmart had the same net worth in 2007 as the bottom 30 percent of Americans. And the phenomenon isn't just limited to the U.S.—income inequality is on the rise in most of the world's major economies, according the Organization of Economic Development and Cooperation.

The high levels of income inequality may help explain why both Rome and America wield so much power. Large wealth gaps actually helped early societies spread, according to an October study. That's because unequal societies crowded out more egalitarian populations, the study found.

Still, the income gap may hurt the U.S. in other ways. A September report from the International Monetary

Fund found that greater income equality positively correlates with stronger economic growth.

Not only that, but it's also unpopular; nearly three-quarters of the respondents in an October poll from *The Hill* said they think income inequality is a problem for the United States. In addition, it's been one of the rallying cries of Occupy Wall Street.

Eleven

Millionaires buy eight-figure properties while foreclosures hit hard in rest of nation

by Alexander Eichler
The Huffington Post, December 21, 2011

IF YOU WANT AN EXAMPLE of how one percenters differ from everyone else, look no further than the housing market.

In a year when a pipeline of foreclosures continued to keep home prices low—and rampant unemployment threatened the stable existence of many a middle class suburbanite—the luxury real estate market was booming, with multimillion-dollar properties in demand in cities around the U.S.

In 2011, buyers purchased a $28 million penthouse in San Francisco, a $31 million townhouse in New York City, and a $100 million mansion in Silicon Valley, the most expensive purchase of a single-family home on record, according to Bloomberg *Businessweek*.

At the same time, U.S. home prices remain near historic lows and a deluge of foreclosures-in-waiting continues to distort the market. In addition, about 15 million homeowners are still underwater—or owe more on their homes than they're worth.

A recent 21 percent quarterly leap in foreclosures only hints at the nationwide extent of the problem: thanks to questionable bookkeeping practices, it's taking longer than it would normally to process the country's countless distressed properties, and prices aren't expected to rise again until the queue is cleared.

The two phenomena—on the one hand, brisk sales of strikingly expensive homes, and, on the other, a lower- and middle-class real estate market showing only minimal signs of life—actually have a similar root cause, according to *Businessweek*. Property values are coming down all over the country, leading wealthy buyers to take advantage of lower prices, even as it throws countless homeowners into debt and pushes them further down the income ladder.

By any measure, affluent Americans have experienced relatively little pain as a result of the housing crash, when compared to the majority of the country. Mid- and low-priced homes have fallen in value by more than 40 percent since 2006, according to a recently analysis from valuation firm Clear Capital, cited by *Time*, while high-priced homes have lost only 26.8 percent of their value.

Analysts and homeowners alike have been waiting for years for the broader housing market to recover.

Despite the occasional positive indicator, prices are still well below healthy market levels, and they're likely to remain depressed as long as millions of foreclosures remain on the books.

A breakdown of November home sales suggests how bleak the financial situation has become for many homeowners. That month, nearly half of all home sales were either short sales—where the borrower's debt exceed the value of the home—or sales of foreclosed homes that had been repossessed by lenders, according to CNN.

Twelve |

The new blue collar: temporary work, lasting poverty and the American warehouse

by Dave Jamieson
The Huffington Post, December 12, 2011

JOLIET, ILL., AND FONTANA, CALIF.,—Like nearly everyone else in Joliet without good job prospects, Uylonda Dickerson eventually found herself at the warehouses looking for work.

"I just needed a job," the 38-year-old single mother says.

Dickerson came to the right place. Over the past decade and a half, Joliet and its Will County environs southwest of Chicago have grown into one of the world's largest inland ports, a major hub for dry goods destined for retail stores through the midwest and beyond. With all the new distribution centers have come thousands of jobs at "logistics" companies—firms that specialize in moving goods for retailers and manufacturers. Many of these jobs are filled by Joliet's African Americans, like Dickerson, and immigrants from Mexico and elsewhere in Latin America.

But many bottom-rung workers like Dickerson don't work for the big corporations whose products are in the warehouses, or even the logistics companies that run them. They go to work for labor agencies that supply workers like Dickerson. Last year, she found work as a temp through one of the myriad staffing agencies that serve big-box retailers and their contractors. Thanks largely to the warehousing boom, Will County has developed one of the biggest concentrations of temp agencies in the midwest.

Dickerson, grateful to have even a temp job, was taken on as a "lumper"—someone who schleps boxes to and from trailers all day long. As unglamorous as her duties were, Dickerson became an essential cog in one of the most sophisticated machines in modern commerce—the Walmart supply chain. Walmart, the world's largest private-sector employer, had contracted a company called Schneider Logistics to operate the warehouse. And Schneider, in turn, had its own contracts with staffing companies that supplied workers.

The experience would change the way Dickerson saw the retail industry—particularly during the frenetic run-up to the holidays, when workers are under tremendous pressure to get products out the door and into stores.

"I don't think people know what the people in these warehouses have to go through to get them their stuff in these stores," Dickerson says. "If you don't work in a warehouse, you don't know."

Dickerson quickly discovered that the work wasn't easy, if there was any work at all. Each morning she showed up at her warehouse, she wasn't sure whether she'd be assigned a trailer and earn a day's pay. She says there were days that she and many temps were told simply to go home, without pay, since there wasn't as much product to unload as expected. Sometimes Dickerson was told they didn't have any trailers light enough for a woman, she says.

But on most days the warehouse teemed with lumpers, many of them wearing different colored t-shirts to signify the different agencies they worked for. Dickerson herself would work for two different labor providers within the same warehouse in a little more than a year.

The difficulty of a lumper's day often went according to chance. A lucky lumper might be assigned a container filled with boxes of Kleenex or stuffed animals, while an unlucky lumper might pull a container filled with kiddie swimming pools, or 200-pound trampolines. For the heaviest lifts, Dickerson would be assigned a partner, and the two would split the pay for the trailer, moving the massive boxes onto pallets by hand.

The job was was fast-paced and stressful. Dickersion says supervisors would walk among the warehouse's bay doors, marking the workers' progress over time. The supervisors, Dickerson and other workers say, often told them to speed it up if they wanted to be invited back. Many of the workers were temps with no job security and no recourse. And the local unemployment rate, then at around 11 percent, promised a long line of potential replacements.

"By the end of the day, your body hurts so bad," says Dickerson, who was among a small minority of females working as lumpers at the warehouse. "You tell them you can't do it the next day, they'll tell you, 'We've got four more people waiting for your job.'"

For a while, Dickerson worked according to "piece rate"—she was not paid by the hour but by the trailer—a stressful pay scheme meant to encourage her and her colleagues to work faster and faster, and one that the labor movement worked hard to abolish in many industries in the 20th century. Each paycheck was different than the last, and most of them were disappointingly low, she says. In her year at the warehouse, Dickerson says she never had health benefits, sick days or vacation days. If she didn't unload containers, she didn't get paid.

"It all depends on how fast you work," she says. "It's like a race. You're racing to get done with the trailer so you can get another one. Otherwise, you won't get enough money."

The warehouse floor wasn't a very welcoming place for a woman, Dickerson says. As one of the relatively few female lumpers, she says she was often fending off crude overtures from male co-workers. And then there were the bathroom issues. While it was piece rate when it benefited the boss, the clock came on for break time. Each day Dickerson had two 15-minute personal breaks in addition to her lunch, but the warehouse was so sprawling—it covered ground equal to several football fields—that it could take her five minutes to walk each way to get some air or use the bathroom, leaving her with only five minuets of personal time.

"When I used to go to the bathroom, I literally had someone counting down the minutes," Dickerson says.

It was particularly difficult when she was on her period and she felt she couldn't use the restroom when she needed to. Eventually, she was being reprimanded for too many breaks, she says. Worried about losing her job, she says she tried so hard to avoid using the bathroom that she eventually developed a bladder infection.

Physically and emotionally drained, Dickerson stopped showing up at the warehouse earlier this year.

"My body still is not the same," she says. "I still have aches and I still have pains. I have migraines because of the stress I went through working at that place."

Dickerson says she's now living in a house where the electricity and water have been shut off, sharing a cell phone with some of her neighbors. She's on government-sponsored health care, just as she was while working at the warehouse, and she now relies on food stamps to get by.

The one place she refuses to take her food stamps is Walmart.

* * *

Walmart may have been the end beneficiary of Dickerson's sweat, but the big-box retailer wasn't directly responsible for her low pay or her aching body. That's one of the many benefits to an employment arrangement based on outsourcing and subcontracting: the corporation at the top indemnifies itself from any unpleasantness at the bottom, thanks to smaller corporate players in the middle. Many American companies have woken up to this fact, with broad implications for the future of blue-collar work.

"It's seems to be spreading like wildfire," Nelson Lichtenstein, a professor of American labor history at the University of California, Santa Barbara, says of such outsourcing, particularly as it relates to temp workers like Dickerson. "All of these companies, wherever they possibly can, they want to create a workforce that doesn't work for them. The question is, *Why? What is the incentive?*

"They're smart," he says, "They run the numbers."

Earlier this year, temporary workers at a Pennsylvania plant packing Hershey products staged a mass walkout over what they described as abusive working conditions. The workers, who were students from Asia and Eastern Europe here on J-1 guest visas for the summer, said they were required to lift 50-pound boxes throughout the day and were threatened with deportation if they couldn't keep up. Although they packed Hershey goods, the students were employed by a staffing company twice removed from Hershey, which had more than $ five billion in revenues last year. Similar outsourcing has spread to much of the American food-packing industry.

But such sub-contracting isn't contained to warehouses and plants. In an effort to cut costs, even hotels have started quietly contracting out a considerable chunk of their back-of-the-house workforce to labor agencies. Hyatt, for example, has replaced many of its housekeepers with cheaper temp workers. Hyatt's direct hires now work alongside many lesser-paid agency workers, some of whom work on a temporary basis for years on end, tracking the minimum wage.

Such subcontracting enables corporations to essentially take workers off their books, foisting the traditional responsibilities that go with being an employer—paying a reasonable wage, offering health benefits, providing a pension or retirement plan, chipping into workers' compensation coverage—conveniently onto someone else. Workers like Dickerson, of course, aren't accounted for when Walmart touts that more than half of its workforce receives health coverage.

As manufacturing jobs continue to head overseas, Americans need new sectors that can provide good, middle-class work for millions of people. Driven as it is by the consumer economy, the retail supply chain should be one of those sectors. But plenty of workers who are lucky enough to have jobs in the industry find themselves earning poverty wages. And while workers get squeezed in the name of lower prices, the overall benefits to consumers may be illusory. By many measures, the middle class is shrinking—and not just because of the Great Recession. There are simply fewer jobs that pay good wages. More than 46 million Americans—roughly one in six—are now living in poverty, the highest number ever recorded by the Census Bureau. Between 2001 and 2007, as the economy boomed, poverty expanded among working-age people for the first time ever during a period of growth. Workers on the whole made less at the end of the boom than they did at the beginning.

In the case of the warehouse industry, where permanent temps are now common, many workers performing the most difficult jobs don't even enjoy the status of basic employees. They work at the pleasure of the agencies employing them. For many of them, getting hurt or slowing down means the end of their gig with no parting compensation—similar to the arrangement detailed in a devastating expose of an American warehouse by the Pennsylvania *Morning Call* in September.

"We have the re-industrialization of American in this distribution nexus," says Lichtenstein. "It's a booming sector of our economy. The kind of work they do is factory labor, and they should be earning (good wages) with benefits. But instead, its insecure and it's low-wage.

"This is the blue-collar working class that should be replacing the steel worker," he said.

* * *

Until a year ago, Debora Terkelson worked in the Costco warehouse, handling boxes of smokes, until she threw her back out moving a heavy load in April, 2010, she says. She worked a few months of light duty but eventually even that proved too painful. No longer able to work, she's now collecting workers' compensation.

"I don't think I'll ever be able to lift again," says Terkelson, 48. "Just doing my laundry each day is a new adventure in pain."

Her life-altering injury notwithstanding, Terkelson had it pretty good by warehouse standards, and in many ways she's lucky to be collecting workers' comp benefits. She says the Costco distribution center is one of the good players in the Inland Empire, an area of southern California that encompasses San Bernardino and Riverside counties and is now home to one of the largest warehouse clusters in the world.

Costco's well-earned reputation for treating its in-store employees well carries over into its warehouse. The Costco warehouse does not reply on temp workers. It hired employees directly. It pays pretty well and it has a safety representative and even stretching classes. Despite all that, the company still manages to provide some of the lowest prices available to customers.

"We tend not to outsource even if we could save money by doing it," says Richard Galanti, Costco's chief financial officer. "We recognize it might cost more but we think it's the right thing to do.... Everyone in the building feels like they're employed."

That attitude makes Costco an outlier in the area, Terkelson says. Her son worked in a nearby shoe warehouse for a temp agency. He came home exhausted each day, with little to show for it, though she guesses the agency made pretty good money off of his work. "They hire them, and as soon as they don't need them, they get rid of them," she says. "They don't care. They treat them like a slave. I'm sorry."

Despite the economic downturn, the Inland Empire is still in the midst of a long-term warehousing boom. Some of the first arrived in the 1990s, when retailers and developers took notice of the area's relatively affordable land and lax regulatory atmosphere. Walmart, Target, Home Depot and Lowe's all picked up warehouse space in the area. They continue to sprout up today, creeping further eastward, some of them with footprints covering more than a million square feet.

As in Joliet, local and politicians in Southern California have hoped warehouse work might replace the decent blue-collar jobs that disappeared with much of the American manufacturing sector in the late decades of the last century. even if we no longer manufacture much in America, we will always need workers to handle all the clothing, electronics, furniture and toys that come here from Asia. And with its proximity to the ports in and around Los Angeles, where the cheap imports from China and elsewhere tend to land, the Inland Empire seemed poised as well as anyone to net a lot of working-class jobs.

There's no doubt that retailers and logistics companies have benefited from the Inland Empire's warehouse boom. The question is whether blue-collar workers have benefitted in kind.

John Husing says they have. An economist who's consulted to local governments dealing with the logistics industry, Husing says "for blue collar workers, the decline in manufacturing shut off their access through that sector to the middle class. In Southern California, in particular, logistics has become an alternative to get to the same place."

Others are less boosterish, including Juan De Lara, an assistant professor at the University of Southern California who's studied the logistics industry in the region. "It's been good to many workers who get paid decent wages for higher-skilled jobs as direct employees," says De Lara. "But it's also been pretty terrible for the workers that work for those temporary agencies."

There are now more than 125,000 direct-hire, full-time jobs in the Inland Empire's logistics industry. Available data makes it difficult to know just how many temp jobs there. Husing doubts it's more than 10,000. Others believe it's several times that number—perhaps even half of all jobs in logistics, according to Warehouse Workers United, a union-backed group that now advocates on behalf of the area's lowest-paid warehouse workers. (Husing dismisses the group's numbers: "The people who throw that stuff around are ideologues. They don't want that sector to survive because they consider it to be dirty.")

The group says the number of temp jobs in the region has skyrocketed in the last two decades, thanks largely to the explosion in the number of warehouses. The industry relies so heavily on temp work that many temp agencies actually have offices inside the warehouses themselves.

Sheheryar Kaoosji, an organizer with Warehouse Workers United, says a decade ago, the ratio of direct hires to temps was 80 percent to 20 percent in many warehouses.

"Now, it's the opposite. and it's accelerated with the (economic) crash," Kasoosji says. "The way that these guys work—the way a Walmart operates—every year they're going to push costs down on each of their contractors. Every year, they're coming back, 'This is going to cost less.' Every year you do that, its going to have an effect. The conditions are going to go down.

"At this point, the wages in some of the facilities have gone down below the federal and state minimums," he says.

*   *   *

With most retailers getting the same products from the same place—i.e., Asia—the supply chain has become one of the few arenas where big-box chains can compete. This competition has led to a tremendous pressure to move goods as quickly as possible. Even the word "warehouse" itself has become something of a misnomer; the idea is no longer to house goods but to keep them moving, from port to rail to tractor-trailer to store display. That's why many warehouses have morphed into what's called a "cross dock": the products come in one side of the warehouse and almost immediately go out the other, barely touching the ground.

Despite modern automation, most warehouses still require bodies, and the pressure to move goods faster and faster often falls on the ones at the bottom. It doesn't help that many of the workers toiling inside the Inland Empire's distribution centers are believed to be undocumented workers from Mexico—a workforce that's generally grateful for whatever pay it can get and far less likely than the American citizen to report workplace abuses, for fear of deportation.

There's plenty of opportunity for exploitation according to charges filed by the California labor department this fall. A company operating in a warehouse handling Walmart goods was allegedly breaking labor law by not providing workers with legitimate earnings statements. Officials allege most of the lumpers were being paid on a piece rate plan that many of them couldn't understand, in what officials have described as a "concentrated effort" to cheat the workers out of their wages. The state issued more than $1 million in fines.

The two labor suppliers cited, Tennessee-based Impact Logistics and North Carolina-based Premier Warehousing, apparently have contracts with Schneider, which, in turn, has a contract with Walmart. Neither Schneider nor Walmart has been accused of any wrongdoing, precisely the outcome the contractor arrangements facilitates.

Julie Su, the California labor commissioner, told HuffPost at the time that the layers of outsourcing can make it nearly impossible to hold big players accountable—a huge collateral benefit in addition to any cost-cutting that goes with subcontracting. "Warehouses are one example of the ever-increasing contracting out of labor," Su said. "It's difficult for enforcement, and in many instances it's a deliberate effort to avoid compliance."

Six lumpers at the warehouse filed a class-action lawsuit on the heels of the state investigation. Everardo Carrillo and his co-workers says they've been moving Walmart goods in a warehouse where the temperature regularly climbs to over 90 degrees, walking in and out of 53-foot-long steel containers that get even hotter baking in the Southern California sun. After working for a set hourly wage, the workers claim that a year and a half ago they were switched to a piece-rate pay plan—an arrangement largely out of a bygone era. Their bosses told them they would actually earn "much more money" under the new scheme, which paid them according to the container, but their earnings actually fell, according to the lawsuit.

The workers claim it was never made clear how their pay was supposed to break down—an allegation apparently bolstered by the state's investigation. They claim that when they complained about their confusing paychecks, their supervisors responded by sending them home without pay or refusing to give them work the next day. The lumpers were working on a temp basis. According to the lawsuit, the majority of workers were direct hires as recently as 2006; now, three out of every four workers are temps.

When asked if a Schneider executive could be interviewed about allegations from temp workers in its warehouses, a spokesperson sent HuffPost a statement, saying its labor suppliers are "separate corporate entities": "The only legal avenue which Schneider had to enforce their companies would be to terminate the contract with these vendors. We have no plans to terminate the contracts with our vendors; our expectation is that they will comply with all applicable statues, regulations and orders."

Walmart, whose products the workers were handling, also kept an arm's length from the charges. When HuffPost reported on the state investigation and lawsuit in October, a Walmart spokesman said the retailer is "not involved in the matter." When a similar lawsuit was filed in April in Illinois—again, naming low-level companies contacted to move Walmart products—the company asserted its distance from the allegations then as well, a spokesman noting that "the facility isn't operated by Walmart nor are the people who work in it employed by Walmart."

In an interview, Walmart spokesman Dan Fogelman declines to say how much of Walmart's logistics work is outsourced, but he says the company has 47 distribution centers across the country, the majority of them owned and operated by Walmart itself. Indeed, the jobs at Walmart's smaller, more regional distribution centers are known to be good, highly coveted jobs. When asked why the company would outsource the work at some of its largest and most important facilities, Fogelman says there are times when a third-party can simply do it better and cheaper.

"Since the early days of our company, the ability to move products quickly and efficiently has really been a driver for our success," Fogelman says. "We're looking for every opportunity to improve our efficiencies. Sometimes that means doing it ourselves; sometimes we're using partners to achieve that.... We're an advocate for our customers. We're doing everything we can to provide them with low prices." As for the allegations from the contracts workers in the Inland Empire and elsewhere, Fogelman says, "We have serious concerns when our contractors or sub-contractors are cited or those types of violations. We hold our contractors to the highest standards."

Ana Sanchez, a 46-year-old from Mexico, says immigrants like her in the Inland Empire inevitably find themselves looking for work at the warehouses. In 2007, Sanchez took a job though a labor agency wrapping and labeling boxes on pallets inside a warehouse she says moved products for Sears and K-Mart, among others. Sanchez was surprised to learn that the work there was as strenuous as it was back in Mexico.

She started at $6.75 an hour and says her wage climbed to more than $8 over time, though it was outstripped by a growing workload. Sanchez' gig required carrying a roll of shrink wrap that, when full, weighed around 50 pounds, and slapping labels on boxes at a dizzying pace; she went through between 5,000 and 8,000 labels on a typical days, she says.

"I would often get the heaviest loads of work because I was so fast," Sanchez says. "Whenever there was a rush order they would call on me because I was two rolls quicker than the other girls."

The job also required a lot of stooping over in tight spaces. One day in 2009, Sanchez threw out her back while working on a rush order. She hoped to be put on light duty or trained for a new, less intensive job, but she says she was being passed back and forth between the company that ran the warehouse and the labor company that she technically worked for. Soon she was fired for allegedly botching an order, she says.

"When you go in to work for a warehouse, you give it your all," she says. "When you get hurt, they treat you as though it doesn't matter."

Sanchez hasn't been able to do manual labor for two years. So what does she do for money?

"I have a lot of friends and relatives who place orders for me to cook tamales," she says with a shrug.

To some people in the Inland Empire, the warehouses have come to represent a dubious bargain. Some good salaries have certainly come with the logistics industry; a directly hired folklift operator, for instance, can expect to make a decent living. But there weren't supposed to be so many temporary positions with measly wages and no benefits. In fact, critics say that temp salaries weren't even figured into the economic projects trotted out by industry boosters and developers who sold the public on the logistics industry. What they did include were the theoretical salaries of unionized warehouse workers and even airplane pilots.

The Inland Empire's thousands of warehouse jobs may also have come at a cost to public health. What used to be diary fields and vineyards two decades ago are now warehouse tracts. Buffeted by mountains to the north and east, and absorbing winds coming from Los Angeles to the west, the Inland Empire has a geological gift for trapping particulate pollution. The area boasted some of the worst air in the country before the logistics boom; residents say it's even worse now.

Mira Loma Village, a community of 1,010 stucco townhouses populated mostly by Latino families, has been hemmed in by warehouses on all sides, with several thousand trucks rolling past the community each day. According to a study done by researchers at the University of Southern California, kids in Mira Loma have abnormally weak lung capacity and slow lung growth. And more warehouses are on their way.

"I see it. I smell it. And I can feel it," Says Laura Borrayo, 42, a Mira Loma resident whose backyard is often coated in a layer of soot from the truck traffic. She says some of the neighborhood children have developed asthma due to the bad air.

Citing some of the worst diesel pollution in the country, Mira Loma residents have filed a lawsuit to stop the latest logistics project—an additional 24 warehouses, covering 1.4 million square feet and expected to bring another 1,555 trucks per day, according to the *L.A. Times*. Residents say the project will occupy what has become the last shred of their buffer zone against the warehouses, taking away their view of the mountains in the process. The lawsuit has put the project on hold for the moment.

Among the residents in Mira Loma Village opposed to more warehouses is Terkelson, the Costco warehouse employee.

"I've lived in this areas for years. When I was a kid, it was beautiful out there," Terkelson says. "But everything went downhill. People don't even realize what they're breathing. The soot, it's nasty. I don't wash my car no more, because it doesn't do no good."

Residents haven't had much luck fighting warehouses in the past, having been cast as opponents of much-needed jobs. Riverside County has an unemployment rate hovering around 14 percent. Penny Newman, director of the Center for Community Action and Environmental Justice, which filed the Mira Loma lawsuit, says the kinds of jobs brought by the warehouses aren't worth the costs.

"There was a lot of fanfare about goods movement being the economic engine of the future," says Newman. "We've discovered that these are not the kinds of jobs anyone should have under the conditions they're facing.... They're temp jobs and they're low-paying and the conditions are bad.

"The money is made by others," Newman says.

* * *

For a lot of the goods that enter the U.S. through the Inland Empire, the next stop is the greater Joliet area, among the largest rail hubs in the country. Within a day's drive of two-thirds of the country, Joliet itself is now home to not one but two massive "intermodal terminals"—the two modes being rail and truck—receiving freight from the West Coast that's then hauled to the area's warehouses and, later, to stores across the U.S.

For one former Teamster who found himself unemployed last year, the growth of the logistics industry in Will County looked like his ticket back into the middle class. Last year this Joliet native, who's in his 50s, responded to an ad in the local paper; a labor agency was bringing in workers to move goods for a major retailer. The firm promises to save its clients on labor costs while simultaneously boosting worker efficiency. (Due to ongoing litigation, neither the worker nor the company will be identified.)

Demonstrating just how booming the logistics industry is in Joliet, the man says the firm was actually sending vehicles out into the community as part of a mobile hiring effort, a bit of proactive recruitment that's hard to find in this economy. He was quickly hired, probably due to his past experience, and to what he pitched as his greatest strength: "I don't miss days."

The fact that this man found himself working as a warehouse temp speaks to his diminished opportunities. He'd been a Teamster for 12 years, driving a truck for a bread company that was eventually shut down, and then for a waste-management company that was relocated to the other side of Chicago, making the commute untenable. It was the kind of good living that's now hard to find. Aside from whatever highly desired jobs remain at the area's lingering refineries, he sees little work outside of the area's new warehouses.

"That's all that's out there," he says.

His trucking experience landed him a pretty cheery gig at the warehouse. He worked primarily as a "spotter," pulling loaded trucks from the bay doors and parking them for the drivers who would take them away to other, smaller distribution centers. He was paid $12 per hour to start, about a buck more than most other new hires, he says. Though he was merely a temp without job security, he considered himself pretty lucky.

"It wasn't a bad job," he says. "It wasn't a bad job."

But about six months in, he says he started to understand how everything worked by design. He was shocked by the warehouse's turnover rate, as new workers constantly came and went, often leaving under bad terms. He guesses the average worker lasted three months, many of them eventually being "pointed out." As in many of Joliet's warehouses, he and his colleagues were working under a demerit system, receiving points for being tardy, missing shifts or not "making rate." Once you hit 10 points, you're gone, he says.

He now argues that workers don't last in part because they're not supposed to. New workers, after all, are cheaper workers. And he also says the little-known temp agencies are there largely to facilitate the churn.

"That's part of the trick—to put as many people between (the retailers) and the actual workers, so they don't have to deal with the actual workers," he says. "They don't have this headache.... They put these temp services between them and the people."

The former Teamster's duties evolved at the warehouse, and eventually he found himself filling online orders to be shipped directly to customers' homes. Working off an order list, he was expected to pick

500 boxes during his 12-hour shift—tight but doable. The problem, he says, is that sometimes the products weren't where they were supposed to be, which cut into his efficiency rate. He says he was supposed to hit a perfect 100 percent each day, but sometimes he dropped into the 90s due to missing products. He clashed with a supervisor over the issue. "How do you expect me to be perfect when the system isn't perfect?" he asks.

One year into his job, he says he was canned after barely missing his rate three days in a row, earning three consecutive writeups—a fireable offense. He wasn't shocked. Having just hit his one-year anniversary, he had become expensive, at least by warehouse standards. His pay has risen to $14 an hour—still not a living wage for the area by some measures, but more than many lumpers will ever see. He had also just started to accrue paid vacation time. Or at least he thought he had.

According to a lawsuit the man filed earlier this year, his company had agreed to give employees one week of paid vacation after they'd worked for the company for a full year. When he was terminated, he was told he'd come up a mere 40 work hours short of earning vacation. But the man says management's tally ignored the considerable overtime he'd worked during the peak season.

The company wouldn't relent, so he and a colleague sued. In addition to the vacation issue they sued the company for not paying working for a minimum of four hours on days they were sent home early or without any work at all, as an Illinois law now mandates. The company denied the allegations.

Like many warehouse workers interviewed for this story, the former Teamster has spent a lot of time wondering how much money the agency made off his work merely for supplying him. The way he sees it, the reliance of Walmart and others on temp agencies is the reason most of the warehouse jobs will never lead to stable living, just the financial anxiety of someone who's temping in perpetuity.

"You can't build on working at these warehouses," he says. "I can't say 'Sweetheart, let's get married. Let's have a baby.' Because I don't know how long it's going to last. I know I'm working now, but will I be working six months from now? And how much money will they screw me out of?"

* * *

The Chicago area has long been home to warehouse jobs, and the vast majority of them used to be decent, blue-collar jobs, says Mark Meinster, international representative with the United Electrical, Radio and Machine Workers of America Union, or UE, which is leading an organizing effort of warehouse workers in Joliet. Meinster says that over the last two decades the jobs have changed along with the retail industry.

With a growing focus on efficiency and cost-cutting within the supply chain, what had been secure and well-paying union jobs are now often low-paying temp jobs, he says. A UE-backed group called Warehouse Workers for Justice interviewed workers at more than 150 area warehouses in 2009, finding that despite plenty of good management positions, about 63 percent of the workers in local warehouses are temps earning less than direct hires. One in four avail themselves of food stamps or welfare, and more than third have to work a second job to make ends meet. (Warehouse Workers for Justice has no affiliation with the California group, Warehouse Workers United.)

"As late as the mid 90s, you saw many warehouse jobs that paid a living wage," says Meinster. "In Chicago, we define that as $15.87 an hour. Now, we're finding that the average wage is somewhere around $9 an hour. Only 4 percent of the workers get sick days. Many are on government assistance. Sixty-two percent are below the poverty line."

John Grueling isn't so bearish. As head of the Will County Center for Economic Development, a non-profit development corporation that did much to attract the industry to Joliet, Grueling says the logistics industry has brought some much-needed jobs to the area as manufacturing has declined. Although he admits that the proliferation of temps is something that concerns him, he says the good jobs outweigh the bad.

"The competition is so severe that they're going to do what they have to do, and in some cases, what they can get away with it," Grueling says of the companies operating in the warehouses. "But we think the industry as whole is very healthy for us." (Grueling says his group no longer tries to lure logistics operations with juicy tax breaks the way they used to.)

Whatever the savings may be, there's another benefit to the subcontracting model for the likes of Walmart: the splintered workforce among all the temp agencies creates a tremendous obstacle to unionization. Plenty of workers who aren't necessarily conspiracy theorists consider it a form of strategic disorganization emanating from down on high. Unionization drives are easily scuttled. When it became apparent that temps were organizing at a Joliet warehouse for vacuum manufacturer Bissell two years ago, the workers soon found themselves out of a job.

Fragmented as they are, dozens of warehouse workers have managed to file class-action lawsuits alleging wage theft in the last couple of years, many of them with the help of a Chicago lawyer named Chris Williams, co-founder of the Working Hands Legal Clinic, which litigates on behalf of low-wage workers. Williams wrote a piece of legislation called the Day and Temporary Labor Services Act, an attempt by Illinois to wrap its hands around the booming and shadowy temp labor industry.

The law requires that labor agencies register with the state and also provide workers with written forms explaining what kind of work they'll be doing and how much they'll be paid for the assignment. Such rudimentary protections are needed, Williams says. He and other worker advocates have discovered fly-by-night temp agencies operating out of area garages, convenience store parking lots and, in one, case, a Super 8 motel room.

In a lawsuit filed last month, 18 workers at the Walmart-contracted warehouse accused a temp company called Eclipse of not paying them the minimum wage and failing to pay them for all the hours they worked. One worker, Roberto Gutierrez, says he worked 21 hours in his first week and was paid a mere $57. On his paystub the company says Gutierrez worked only 12.5 hours, though by their math he still doesn't seem to have been earning the minimum wage. According to another lawsuit, one of the temp agencies charged applicants for their own employment background checks; when the cost was deducted from their first checks, it pushed their pay below the minimum age. Such lawsuits are fast becoming a cost of doing business for the temp companies.

"There's a huge problem with people being shorted," says Williams. "In aggregate, it's millions and millions in savings" for the companies.

So far, most of the energy from gadflies like Williams has been devoted to the Walmart supply chain. Like others, Williams argues that Walmart has trailblazed the temp worker model within the retail world, and that other major retailers are simply following its path, as they often do.

None of the lawsuits involving the Walmart warehouse have touched Walmart itself. By the way Illinois' temp labor law was written, a company at the top of a contracting tree could feasibly be held accountable for abuses at the bottom. In one case, Williams discovered that there were four companies separating Walmart from the workers who were handling Walmart goods at the warehouse.

"I believe Walmart is experimenting," Williams says. Of the area's warehouses generally, he adds, "You see temp agencies that supervise temp agencies that deal with temp agencies. It just adds another level of distance."

According to worker Demetrie Collins, the presence of temp companies has been growing just as the conditions and pay have been deteriorating. Collins says he earned a pretty good wage running a forklift at one of the warehouses five hears ago. Then, after a break from work and a prison stint for a drug charge, he says he returned at the warehouses to see temp workers everywhere. He got on as a lumper at a warehouse but was fired earlier this year, he says. Unemployed, he now volunteers at the Warehouse Workers for Justice.

"Hell, yeah, there's more temp agencies," says Collins. "Used to be they'd pay you good. But now, the warehouses are paying you shitty, and there's nothing you can do about it. Fire them today, temp agencies gonna replace them tomorrow. They can treat the workers however they want to treat them."

The downsides of temping go well beyond lower wages and fewer benefits. Many workers have to call in to the warehouse each morning to see if they still have a job for the day, essentially making them job-seekers-in-perpetuity. The supplication can be demoralizing. One former lumper told HuffPost his temp status once cost him a loan—from a payday lender. The lender apparently thought he posed too great a risk, seeing as he had no guarantee on his employment from week to week.

Meinster, of the UE, says the temp system creates an entire tier of workers who are basically second-class.

"Despite the fact that these workers are paid poverty-level wages, we estimate that about a trillion dollars comes through Chicago on an annual basis," says Meinster. "That's about $6 million per warehouse worker. Each worker is responsible for moving $6. million worth of goods through that supply chain. These are the workers who, collectively, if they don't show up for a day, these companies would stand to lose a lot of money.

"That's something these companies need to pay attention to," he says.

* * *

A few months ago, the former Teamster heard of about 50 job openings at the warehouse for Central Foods, a food wholesaler based in Joliet. The positions were similar to ones at the warehouse where he'd temped, but the pay and benefits seemed to be from another world. The Central Foods jobs were union jobs, starting out at a livable $16. an hour, with good health coverage, an annual raise a 402(k) and a chance to make as much as $24 an hour after a few years, he says.

"What was the difference?" the former Teamster asks rhetorically. "No temp service."

Unfortunately, word about the direct-hire jobs and apparently spread throughout Joliet, with the competition so fierce that it made the local news. "Here they have health benefits and a pension," one man told the Joliet *Herald-News* in wonderment. "I never had a job that could do that for me." Another applicant bemoaned all the temp warehouses jobs on his resume. "It makes me look like a job hopper, but I'm not," he said.

When the former Teamster arrived to apply, scores of eager jobs seekers were already there, with a line coming out the door and snaking around the corner, Ultimately, more than a thousand people threw their hats in the ring, many of them boasting previous warehouse experience. The former Teamster waited nearly three hours to put in his application and make his trusty pitch: "I don't miss days."

Must be a great gig if you can get it, he thought.

Post script:
Purple Hearts,
Christmas ...
and Santayana

ONE OF THE MOST POIGNANT recent articles was published in the Holland, Michigan, *Sentinel* in mid-December, 2011.

It described how one serviceman, on leave, went to the A-Z Outlet pawn shop in Holland and pawned one of his two Purple Hearts. He earned them after he was wounded in Afghanistan, the newspaper reported.

The Purple Heart is America's highest decoration—awarded for being wounded or killed in action against an enemy.

"He was falling on hard times," Bryan VanderBosch, owner of the pawn shop, told the *Sentinel*. "He said the same thing everyone else who comes in here says. He was short on funds."

"Despite their service to the country," the *Sentinel* said, "veterans struggle more than most. The veteran unemployment rate in Michigan (in late 2011) was almost 30 percent, triple the state's overall unemployment rate and higher than that of any other state."

The serviceman declined to be interviewed for the Holland *Sentinel's* article.

To his credit, the pawn shop owner, VanderBosch, said he would not re-sell the Purple Heart. He said he would hold it for the serviceman and sell it back at the purchase price, without interest.

George Santayana was born in Madrid, Spain, in 1863; he was educated at Harvard University and taught philosophy at Harvard. He left the United States at 48, returned to Europe, and died in Rome, at 88, in 1952. One of his most famous quotations appeared in his book *Reason in Common Sense* (1905):

> *Those who cannot remember the past*
> *are condemned to repeat it.*

References

Chapter 1

Page

1 "They gave me stories to cover ..." Benson, *The True Adventures of John Steinbeck, Writer,* pp. 95.

2 "which were commercial failures ..." Fensch, *Steinbeck and Covici: The Story of a Friendship,* pp. 9.

2 "but only 598 copies ..." St. Pierre, *John Steinbeck: The California Years,* pp. 57.

3 "*Tortilla Flat* was an immediate hit ..." Fensch, "Introduction," *Tortilla Flat,* Penguin Books, 1997, pp. xiii.

4 "His fame grew rapidly ..." Benson, *The True Adventures ...* , pp. 120.

4 "In the mid-thirties ..." St. Pierre, pp. 60–61.

6   "One of the tactics ..." Benson, pp. 303-304.

6   "In life ..." Ibid., 306.

7   Paradise Lost ... *John Steinbeck: Novels and Stories, 1932–1937*, pp. 531. Steinbeck novels with ancient or biblical themes: *Tortilla Flat*, the King Arthur and the Knights of the Round Table saga; *Of Mice and Men*, from the Old Testament, "Am I my brother's keeper?"; *The Grapes of Wrath*, the journey of the Tribe of Israel from their land of bondage (Egypt) toward their own promised land; *East of Eden*, the Cain/Abel story.

7   "He had, in fact, based the book, ..." *Ibid.*, pp. 12.

7   "Eventually Steinbeck was disappointed ..." Lisca, pp. 68.

8   "The novel's action ..." *Ibid.*, pp. 64–65.

9   "This is the best set-up ..." *In Dubious Battle*, in *John Steinbeck, Novels and Stories, 1932–1937*, pp. 625.

10   "... the growers ..." Benson, pp. 305-306.

10   "You think we're too important ..." *John Steinbeck, Novels and Stories, 1932–1937*, pp. 776.

11   "the growers and ..." Benson, pp. 307-308.

12   "London handed the lantern up ..." *John Steinbeck: Novels and Stories, 1932–1937*, pp. 793.

Chapter 2

Page

14   "Their exodus ..." Benson, pp. 335.

15   "The first camp ..." St. Pierre, pp. 76-77.

17   "Guided by Lange ..." David Roberts, "Travels with Steinbeck," *American Photographer*, March, 1989, pp. 45.

19   "Most of Steinbeck's best work ..." St. Pierre, pp. 77.

19   "In preparation for his trip ..." Benson, pp. 332. Hoovervilles were migrant or hobo camps, usually built from cardboard or other such materials and named after Herbert Hoover, who was president during the early years of the stock market crash and the Great Depression. Many citizens throughout the country believed he had no idea at all about how to correct the Great Depression; thus the ironic name for their squatter shacks.

21   "At this season of the year ..." *John Steinbeck: The Harvest Gypsies: On the Road to the Grapes of Wrath.* Introduction by Charles Wollenberg, pp.19. All citations from *The Harvest Gypsies* are from the Wallenberg edition.

23   "The next door neighbor family ..." *Ibid.*, pp. 29-30.`

23   "wattling weeds ..." this is probably a misprint and should be *wadding* or jamming weeds ...

23 "It will not turn water at all ..." i.e.; is not a roof.

25 "The family Steinbeck was writing about ..." Benson, *The True Adventures* ... , pp. 334.

26 "It is rare...." Steinbeck, *The Harvest Gypsies*, pp. 34.

27 "takes part in ..." *Ibid.*, pp. 40.

27 "When a new family enters ..." *Ibid.*, 41.

28 "New arrivals ..." *Ibid.*, pp. 42.

28 "The case histories ..." *Ibid.*, pp. 46-48.

28 "Family of eight ..." *Ibid.*, pp. 49.

29 "The following is an example: ..." *Ibid.*, pp. 50-51.

30 "By 1920 ..." *Ibid.*, pp. 53.

30 "Between 1920 and 1929 ..." *Ibid.*, pp. 55.

30 "Foreign labor is ..." *Ibid.*, pp. 57.

31 "The California Attorney General's Office ..." *Ibid.*, pp. 57.

32 "'The Harvest Gypsies' (were) ..." Robert DeMott ed., *Working Days: The Journals of The Grapes of Wrath*, pp. xxxiv-xxxv.

32 "When they were first published ..." *Ibid.*, pp. xxxv.

32 "From his numerous field trips ..." Ibid., pp. xli-xlii.

Chapter 3

Page

36   "He pointed in the case ..." Steinbeck, *The Grapes of Wrath*, 1939 edition, *pp.* 218-219.

37   "A short heavy man ..." *Ibid.*, pp. 527.

38   "Then what, Tom?" *Ibid.*, pp. 572.

39   "A blue shriveled little mummy." *Ibid.*, pp. 603.

39   "In the gray dawn light ..." *Ibid.*, pp. 609.

41   "Each stage varied in audience ..." DeMott, ed, *Working Days*, pp. xxxiii.

42   "There was ... something ..." Benson, *The True Adventures ...* , pp. 375.

42   "protesting what I had seen ..." Steinbeck, in *Working Days*, pp. lv.

42   "The owners of the land ..." Steinbeck, *The Grapes of Wrath*, pp. 43; "the bank, the monster ..." pp. 44.

45   "Sure, cried the tenant men ..." pp. 45.

46   "Few novelists ..." Benson, *The True Adventures ...* , pp. 418.

46   "I say to you ..." Boren, quoted in Benson, pp. 418-419.

46   "Obscene in the extreme ..." Rick Wartzman, *Obscene in the Extreme: The Burning and Banning of John Steinbeck's* The Grapes of Wrath.

46   "Let me tell you a story ..." Fensch, *Steinbeck and Covici*, pp. 21.

47   "Twenty-two years later ..." Thomas Fensch, *The Man Who Changed His Skin: The Life and Work of John Howard Griffin*, pp. 107.

47   "... beat him with chains," *Ibid.*, pp. 116.

48   "There is a crime here ..." Steinbeck, *The Grapes of Wrath*, pp. 477. Pellagra is a vitamin B3 deficiency.

Suggested readings

"America's Youngest Outcasts 2010." Needham, Mass.: The National Center on Family Homelessness, 2011.

Benson, Jackson. *The True Adventures of John Steinbeck, Writer*. New York: The Viking Press, 1984.

Blumenkranz, Carla, et al. *Occupy! Scenes from Occupied America*. London and New York: Verso, 2011.

Chafkin, Max. "Revolution Number 99," *Vanity Fair*, Feb., 2012.

DeParle, Jason. "Harder for Americans to Rise From Lower Rungs," *The New York Times*, Jan. 4, 2012.

Dewan, Shalia. "As Wars End, Young Veterans Return to Scant Jobs," *The New York Times*, Dec. 18, 2011.

Fensch, Thomas. "Introduction," *Tortilla Flat*. New York: Penguin Books, 1997.

_____. *The Man Who Changed His Skin: The Life and Work of John Howard Griffin*. Richmond: New Century Books, 2011.

_____. *Steinbeck and Covici: The Story of a Friendship*. Middlebury, Vt.: Paul S. Eriksson, Publisher. 1979.

Friedman, Thomas and Michael Mandelbaum. *That Used to Be Us: How America Fell Behind in the World It Invented and How We Can Come Back*. New York: Farrar, Straus and Giroux, 2011.

Lewis, Michael. *Panic: The Story of Modern Financial Insanity*. New York: W.W. Norton Co., 2009.

Lisca, Peter. *John Steinbeck: Nature and Myth*. New York: Thomas Crowell Co., 1978.

Maharidge, Dale. *Someplace Like America: Tales from the New Great Depression*. Berkeley, Calif.: The University of California Press, 2011.

Steinbeck, John. *The Grapes of Wrath*. New York: The Viking Press, 1939.

_____. *The Harvest Gypsies*. Berkeley: Heydey Books, 1988.

_____. *In Dubious Battle*. New York: Covici-Friede, 1936.

_____. *Working Days: The Journals of* The Grapes of Wrath, *1938–1941*. New York: The Viking Press, 1989.

Stiglitz, Joseph. "The Book of Jobs," *Vanity Fair*, Jan., 2012.

St. Pierre, Brian. *John Steinbeck: The California Years*. San Francisco: Chronicle Books, 1983.

Wartzman, Rick. *Obscene in the Extreme: The Burning and Banning of John Steinbeck's* The Grapes of Wrath. New York: Public Affairs Press, 2008.

About the author ...

THOMAS FENSCH HAS HAD a life-long love affair with the printed word.

He is the author of four previous books about John Steinbeck. His first, *Steinbeck and Covici: The Story of a Friendship*, which analyzed Steinbeck's relationship with his editor-publisher Pascal Covici, was widely reviewed. It is now considered one of the seminal books in Steinbeck scholarship. He has lectured about Steinbeck in the U.S. and in Japan.

He is also the author of books about: James Thurber; Theodor "Dr. Seuss" Geisel; Ernest Hemingway; Oskar Schindler and John Howard Griffin and has published other books of nonfiction.

He has a doctorate from Syracuse University and is a member of the faculty of Virginia Union University, Richmond. He lives outside Richmond, with his four literary advisors, Sally, a Great Pyrenees, Wolfie, a white German Shepherd, Charlie, a Labradoodle and Miss Gypsy, a Goldendoodle.

www.ingramcontent.com/pod-product-compliance
Lightning Source LLC
Chambersburg PA
CBHW060757050426
42449CB00008B/1432